WHY DO WE SAY THAT?

404 Idioms, Phrases, Sayings & Facts! An English Idiom
Dictionary To Become A Native Speaker By Learning
Colloquial Expressions, Proverbs & Slang

SCOTT MATTHEWS

The more that you read, the more things you will know.

The more you learn, the more places you'll go.

- Dr. Seuss

Contents

Introduction

Are you ready to explore the intriguing world of idioms? You might be surprised to learn that we use them daily, sometimes without even realizing it! But have you ever wondered about the origins of these fascinating phrases?

Also called idiomatic expressions, idioms have slowly been introduced into the English language as it has developed over time. These expressions have a commonly understood meaning which varies from the literal meaning of the words being spoken, read, or written.

As we explore the origins of idioms, we'll be taking a journey back in time to discover what the English-speaking world was like when these phrases were first used. While some idioms have clear origins, others have evolved over time, passed down through oral tradition, and may have unknown origins or multiple theories of where they came from. Despite this, the enduring popularity and widespread use of these idioms continue to pique our interest and inspire further inquiry.

So let's dive right into the wonderful world of idioms and where they come from!

1. Skeleton in the closet

The phrase "skeleton in the closet" conjures up imagery of a dark, personal secret hidden away from the public eye, much like a literal skeleton concealed behind closed doors. The idiom's origins are shrouded in historical mystery, but two prominent theories offer intriguing backstories.

The first theory takes us back to the anatomy classrooms of the 19th century. At that time, the study of medical science was booming, and the demand for cadavers for dissection was at an all-time high. However, the supply was not always legally sourced, and some anatomists resorted to underhanded methods to obtain specimens— sometimes even body-snatching. It's believed that some medical professionals kept illegally obtained skeletons hidden in closets, away from prying eyes, thus giving rise to the saying.

Another origin story is more allegorical, dating back even further. It refers to the domestic practice in many old European households of keeping family heirlooms and secrets hidden away in storage rooms or closets. The 'skeleton' represents the grim or scandalous family histories that were not to be revealed to outsiders, symbolizing the idea of family shame or sin that could tarnish a family's reputation if exposed.

Today, to have a "skeleton in the closet" means to have an embarrassing or potentially damaging secret from the past that one wishes to keep undisclosed. This idiom underscores the universal human theme of secrecy and the fear of past mistakes or misdeeds being uncovered.

2. Cry over spilled milk

The idiom "cry over spilled milk" is an expression that means to complain or grieve over something that has already happened and cannot be changed. The origin of the phrase comes from the fact that crying over spilled milk is considered a pointless and futile action, as the milk is already spilled and cannot be recovered, and is often prefaced with "there's no use crying over spilled milk." The phrase was first seen in 1659 by writer and historian James Howell in one of his works, *Paramoigraphy*.

3. Behind the scenes

The idiom "behind the scenes" has its roots in theater. It originally referred to the area behind the stage where actors and crew prepare for a performance. The colloquial phrase has been used since at least the early 19th century to refer to actions or activities that take place out of public view. The phrase has a metaphorical meaning, referring to the unseen work that goes into creating something or making something happen.

4. Keep your eyes peeled

There are two origin stories linked to this idiom. Firstly, when someone peels an orange, they remove its skin and open it up. So to "keep your eyes peeled" means keeping the skin, or eyelids, off your eyes, ensuring that they are open. The second origin story goes back to the founding of the Metropolitan Police Force in London in 1829. Sir Robert Peel, the Home Secretary at the time, founded the force, and policemen were quickly nicknamed 'bobbies' or 'peelers,' both derived from his name. Peelers kept watch on unsavory characters, and while the nickname has faded into obscurity, the idiom lives on. Today, to "keep your eyes peeled" is used more broadly to mean to be on the lookout or pay close attention to something, particularly to be ready for any potential challenges or opportunities. It is often used to express a sense of vigilance or alertness and the need to be prepared for whatever may come.

5. Separate the wheat from the chaff

The phrase "separate the wheat from the chaff" means to set apart valuable or useful things from less valuable or useful ones. This saying originates from the agricultural practice of separating the wheat kernels from the inedible chaff (the dry, scaly protective coverings of cereal grain) using a process called winnowing. This was done by throwing the mixture of wheat and chaff into the air on a windy day, and the chaff would blow away while the heavier wheat kernels would fall back to the ground. It has its origins in the Bible as a metaphor that speaks about how God will separate those who are worthy and those who are unworthy. In the Bible, it is written, "His winnowing fork is in his hand, and he will clear his threshing floor, gathering his wheat into the barn and burning up the chaff with unquenchable fire." This metaphor was used to explain how the good will be rewarded and the bad will be punished. In modern times, it might refer to a sport where the upper echelon is clearly better than the rest.

6. Cool as a cucumber

The idiom "cool as a cucumber" is used to describe someone who remains calm and composed during difficult or stressful situations. It originated in the early 18th century, likely from the physical properties of cucumbers which have a cool and refreshing temperature when cut open due to their high water content (which can be as high as 96%). The term is often used to describe someone level-headed and able to maintain composure in the face of adversity. The original meaning of the word "cool" in the phrase referred to self-confident and calm, which was first written in a verse by British poet John Gay in his 1732 poem *New Song on New Similies*: "Cool as a cucumber could see the rest of womankind."

7. Egg on your face

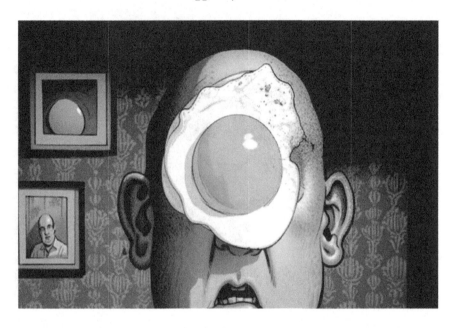

The idiom "egg on your face" is a colloquial expression that denotes being embarrassed or humiliated, often as a result of one's own actions or words. The origin of this American idiom is unknown. One possible source of the phrase can be traced back to popular theater during the 1800s and early 1900s, where sub-par actors would often be pelted with rotten vegetables and eggs, resulting in them having egg on their faces. Another possible origin stems from the farmyard, where farm dogs sometimes develop a taste for eggs. To identify the culprit, a farmer may look for the egg on the dog's face as a sign of guilt. The metaphor suggests that one is embarrassed or humiliated, much like an actor might feel embarrassed if they had egg on their face, or a dog might feel guilty if it had egg on its face. The earliest written record of this phrase dates back to the early 20th century, in a book called *The American Language* by H.L. Mencken, published in 1919, where it is defined as "to be embarrassed or humiliated, often as a result of one's own actions or words."

8. Sit tight

The phrase "to sit tight" means to remain in a passive or inactive position and wait for something to happen, rather than taking action. It can also mean to remain in a particular situation, often a difficult or challenging one, and not make any changes. It is often used to suggest that someone should not act impulsively or take unnecessary risks, but instead wait for a more favorable outcome. The term originated in the early 20th century, and was used in the context of stock market investments, suggesting that investors should not panic and sell their stocks during a market downturn, but instead hold on to them and wait for the market to recover.

9. Neck and neck

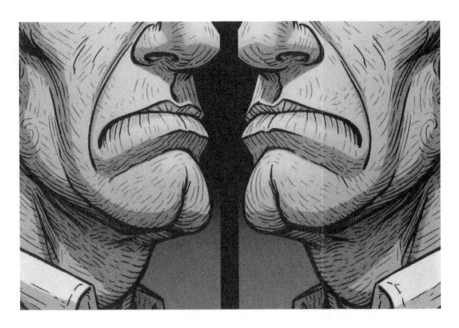

The idiom "neck and neck" has its roots in horse racing. The phrase was first recorded in the early 1800s and was used to describe a close race where the winning horse "won by a neck." This is because during a tight race, what is often observed are the horses running side by side, with their necks stretched out as they compete to be the first to cross the finish line. Thus, the commentator is often heard saying "they were neck and neck, but the distance between the winning horse and the second horse was a neck."

10. Wild goose chase

The term "wild goose chase" refers to a futile or pointless pursuit or search. It is often used to describe a situation in which someone is trying to achieve or find something that is unlikely to be successful. The origins of this idiom can be traced back to the 16th century, when it was used to describe a type of horse race in which riders followed a leader, who was often depicted as a goose. The leader would lead the riders on a serpentine route, and the riders would follow as closely as possible. The phrase "wild goose chase" was first recorded in this context in the book *The Art of Horsemanship* by the English poet Gervase Markham, which was published in 1593. The idiom is also mentioned in the play *Romeo and Juliet* by William Shakespeare. In Act 2, Scene 4, the character Mercutio uses the phrase to describe the pursuit of a woman. He says, "Nay, if our wits run the wild-goose chase, I am done; for thou hast more of the wild goose in one of thy wits than, I am sure, I have in my whole five."

Did You Know?

You might notice that a lot of idioms are derived from gambling. This is because gambling has been a popular pastime for centuries and has played an important role in many cultures. In the past, gambling was not just a form of entertainment but also a way to make a living.

Gambling is often associated with risk and uncertainty, and many idioms that come from gambling reflect this. For example, "to bet on a long shot" means to take a risk on something unlikely to happen, while "to hedge your bets" means to protect yourself from potential losses by making multiple bets.

Additionally, gambling often involves using metaphors related to money, such as "ante up," meaning to put money in the pot, and "to cash in" meaning to take your winnings. Gambling also often involves expressions of chance and luck, such as "to roll the dice," meaning to take a chance, or "to play your cards right," meaning to make the best of the situation.

Gambling also has a long history of being a social activity and, in many cases, idioms that come from gambling reflect this aspect. Gambling idioms are often used in the context of making a decision or taking a risk or making a bet, which is why they are often used in everyday life beyond the gambling context. Some of the oldest games dating back to ancient times:

1. Dice games: Dice games have been around since ancient times, with evidence of dice usage dating back to 6000 BC. Dice games were popular among the ancient Greeks, Romans, and Egyptians. These games involved rolling dice to determine the outcome and were played for both entertainment and financial gain.

2. Keno: Keno is a Chinese lottery game that dates back to around 200 BC. The game involves picking numbers and betting on the outcome of a drawing, much like modern-day lottery games. Keno was used as a way to raise funds for the state and it remains a popular form of gambling in many countries.

3. Chaupar/Pachisi: Chaupar, also known as Pachisi, is a board game from ancient India that is considered a precursor to modern-day parcheesi. The game involves moving pieces around a board based on the roll of dice, and was played by Indian royalty. It was considered a symbol of wealth and status.

4. Hnefatafl: Hnefatafl is a Scandinavian board game from the Viking Age that was played for both entertainment and gambling purposes. The game involves moving pieces on a board to capture the opponent's king and was played by both common people and royalty.

5. Hazard: Hazard is an English game of chance that was played with dice and is considered one of the earliest forms of the modern day game of craps. The game involved betting on the outcome of dice rolls and was played by royalty and commoners alike. Hazard was introduced to the American colonies and became popular in the United States, where it evolved into the game of craps that is played today.

6. Chess: Chess has been played for over a thousand years by people of all social classes and was considered a symbol of intelligence and strategy.

11. The apple of one's eye

The idiom "the apple of one's eye" is used to describe someone who is greatly valued or cherished. The phrase originates from the Bible, specifically in Deuteronomy 32:10 where it is written, "He found him in a desert land, and in the waste howling wilderness; he led him about, he instructed him, he kept him as the apple of his eye." This phrase is a metaphor that compares someone to the pupil of the eye, which is considered precious and protected. Often, "the apple of one's eye" refers to a loved one whom the speaker values above all others.

12. Pigeonhole

The term "pigeonhole" has a rich history dating back to the late 1500s, where it was originally used to describe a small recess for pigeons to nest in. This bird box-like shape can still be seen in modern units today. During medieval times, farmers and those in the agriculture trade commonly utilized pigeonholes to keep domestic birds for their families' consumption, which were also referred to as dovecotes and closely resembled tiny houses for birds to nest in. In the late 1700s, the term "pigeonhole" was adopted to describe office furniture used for housing and organizing paperwork, due to their close resemblance to the domestic pigeonholes. Today, pigeonholes are still widely used in schools and businesses around the world, particularly in mailrooms as they greatly improve the organization of mail that needs to be manually sorted.

13. On the line

The idiom "on the line" refers to something that is at risk, often in a high-pressure or high-stakes situation. Some sources suggest that the term may have originated as early as the end of the 17th century, while others suggest that it may have originated as late as the 1940s. It is possible that the phrase has evolved over time and has been used in a variety of different contexts, including aboard British naval vessels, in gambling dens, and to describe urgency in a tense situation.

14. Hit the nail on the head

"Hit the nail on the head" is a common saying that refers to the precise identification or core essence of something. Additionally, it may also connote the successful resolution of a problem or the provision of a correct solution. The phrase is derived from carpentry, where the analogy is straightforward: when hammering in a nail, striking the head is crucial and failure to do so may result in damage to the surface or even injury. In casual conversation, a person might express something in a way that resonates with you or perfectly encapsulates a point, and you could rightly say that they "hit the nail on the head."

15. Your guess is as good as mine

"Your guess is as good as mine" refers to a situation in which someone does not have any more information or knowledge than the other person. It originated in the 19th century and is derived from the idea of making an educated guess or estimation about something based on the available information. Today, the phrase is used to convey a sense of uncertainty or lack of knowledge.

16. We're not in Kansas anymore

The saying "we're not in Kansas anymore" is used to describe a situation in which someone is in a very different place or circumstances than they are used to. It is often used to describe a person who has left their familiar surroundings and is now in a new or unfamiliar environment. The phrase "we're not in Kansas anymore" is a reference to the 1939 film *The Wizard of Oz*, in which the main character, Dorothy, is transported from her home in Kansas to the fantastical land of Oz. In the film, Dorothy repeatedly says "we're not in Kansas anymore" as a way of expressing her surprise and disorientation as she travels the land and meets all sorts of strange people and creatures.

17. Up a creek without a paddle

The idiom "up a creek without a paddle" refers to a situation in which someone is in a difficult or problematic position and lacks the means or resources to extricate themselves. It originated in the 19th century and is derived from the idea of being in a small boat or canoe without a paddle, which would make it difficult or impossible to steer or move the boat. Today, the phrase is used to convey a sense of helplessness or perhaps to note that the person in the predicament should have been better prepared.

18. Dead end job

A "dead end job" is commonly used to describe employment that has limited or no potential for advancement or professional growth. These types of jobs are often characterized by low wages and unsatisfying work that does not provide a clear trajectory for career development or fulfillment for the employee. The expression has its origins in the early 20th century, and is thought to have been derived from the term "dead end," which was first used in the 1880s to describe a blocked water pipe. By the 1920s, it had evolved into an idiom meaning a situation with no way out.

19. Up in the air

The idiom "up in the air" is used to describe a situation that is uncertain, unresolved, or in a state of flux. The term is often used when a plan hasn't been settled on or where there is a lack of clarity or certainty about an outcome from an endeavor. The phrase "up in the air" has been in use since the early 20th century, and it most likely originated from the literal meaning of something being in the air, such as an airplane or a balloon. In the early 20th century, airplanes were new technology, and the idea of something being "up in the air" was associated with the uncertainty and unpredictability of flight. It is also possible that the phrase has origins in nautical terminology, where ships at anchor in a port, ready for departure and with sails opened, are said to be "up in the air."

20. Look before you leap

The idea that one should "look before you leap" refers to the importance of considering the potential consequences of one's actions before making a decision or taking the first step. It is thought to have originated in the 16th century and is likely derived from the idea of looking before jumping to avoid danger. It can be used to describe a wide range of situations, from casual conversation to life-changing decisions. Today, the phrase is often used to convey a sense of caution or prudence, where another person might warn you to "look before you leap" into a fraught situation.

Did You Know?

Many idioms come from famous poets, philosophers, and writers from the past. This is because they were some of the most well-known and respected figures of their time, and their words and phrases were widely read and shared. They often wrote about the human experience and used vivid and imaginative language to convey their ideas. These phrases and expressions were used by the general population, and over time they became a part of everyday language and culture. Additionally, literature and poetry were more prevalent in the past and people were more likely to be exposed to them, which also played a role in idioms becoming a part of everyday language. Furthermore, many of these writers were trying to convey complex ideas in simple ways, which made their language and phrases more memorable and useful for everyday use.

Some famous poets, philosophers, and writers who have contributed idioms to the English language include:

William Shakespeare: Shakespeare is widely considered one of the greatest writers in the English language and many of his plays and poems are still widely read and performed today. Many idioms and phrases that we use nowadays come from his works, such as "to be or not to be," "the world is your oyster," and "good riddance."

George Orwell: George Orwell is best known for his books *1984* and *Animal Farm*. Phrases like "big brother" and "doublethink" originated from his book *1984*.

Benjamin Franklin: Benjamin Franklin was a statesman, scientist, and writer, and is known for his famous idioms like "a penny saved is a penny earned."

Confucius: Confucius is a Chinese philosopher, his teachings and sayings have been widely known and used, idioms like "Confucius say."

Mark Twain: Mark Twain, an American writer and humorist, is known for his famous idioms like "the truth is stranger than fiction."

Socrates: Socrates is considered one of the founders of Western philosophy. The phrase "the Socratic method" refers to a method of teaching and learning through asking questions and engaging in dialogue.

Aristotle: Aristotle was a student of Plato and tutored Alexander the Great, he wrote on various subjects including his book *Rhetoric*, and his name is associated with terms like "Aristotelian logic" and "Aristotelian syllogism."

Plato: Plato was a student of Socrates and a teacher of Aristotle, he wrote many *Dialogues*, and some of the most famous idioms that come from Plato's works include "Platonic love" and "Plato's cave."

21. Whet one's appetite

The phrase "whet one's appetite" means to stimulate or increase interest in something. It is often used with a teaser or appetizer to something much larger and grander, like an idea or product, that is trying to hook the target audience to go further. The word "whet" means to sharpen or make more keen, and in this context, describes how something can sharpen or increase one's desire for something. This phrase is usually used in relation to food to describe something that has made someone more hungry or eager to eat. However, it can also be used more broadly to describe anything that has increased someone's interest or desire. The origin of this idiom is not clear, but it's been used since the early 19th century.

22. Straw man

The term "straw man" refers to a rhetorical device where an argument or opponent's position is misrepresented or distorted in order to make it appear weaker or more easily refutable than it actually is. This is often used in debates, political discussions, and other forms of discourse as a way of discrediting an opposing viewpoint. The origins of the term "straw man" are traced back to the early 19th century when it was used in legal contexts. When a person was unable to pay a debt, a straw man would be used as a front for the debtor, with the straw man taking on the debt in their name. This would allow the debtor to avoid paying the debt and the creditor to avoid losing the money. The phrase "man of straw" is also related to the straw man concept, and it's used to describe a person who is weak, insubstantial, or easily swayed. The phrase is thought to have originated from the practice of using a straw man as a front for a debtor, as a straw man is seen as weak and insubstantial.

23. Deer in the headlights

The saying "deer in the headlights" refers to someone who is surprised or stunned by something and is unable to react or respond. The bright lights of a car can cause a deer to freeze in place, unable to move or react, and this is similar to the way that a person might freeze or become unable to react when faced with something unexpected or frightening. The earliest written use of this phrase dates back to the mid-20th century. It appears in the book *The New Dictionary of American Slang* by Harold Wentworth and Stuart Berg Flexner, which was published in 1960.

24. Go over with a fine tooth comb

The phrase "go over with a fine-tooth comb" is an expression that means to examine something very carefully or thoroughly. The origins come from the practice of using a comb with fine teeth to comb through hair or fibers to remove tangles or debris. The term originated in the late 19th century and has been used to describe the act of scrutinizing something with great attention to detail. It is also used to describe the process of searching for something specific or identifying errors or problems in a detailed manner.

25. Dark horse

The term "dark horse" is an expression that refers to a person (or a group, idea, technology, etc.) that is unexpected or unknown, but has the potential to become successful. The origin of the phrase comes from horse racing, specifically, a horse that is not well-known or has not previously competed, but has the potential to win the race. The phrase originated in the early 19th century, with the earliest known reference to the phrase in Benjamin Disraeli's novel *The Young Duke* in 1831, where he wrote: "A dark horse, which had never been thought of... rushed past the grandstand in sweeping triumph."

26. Cheapskate

The word "cheapskate" is a derogatory term used to describe someone who is excessively frugal or miserly. It suggests that the person is unwilling to spend money or is always looking for ways to save or cut costs, even when it is not necessary. There are a few theories about the origin of the word "cheapskate." One possibility is that it originated from the combination of the words "cheap" and "skate," which were both used to describe someone who was dishonest or unreliable. In this context, a "cheapskate" might be someone who was dishonest or unwilling to pay their fair share. Another theory is that it evolved from the phrase "cheap skate," which referred to a type of shoe that was made of cheap materials and was prone to falling apart. In this context, someone who was a "cheapskate" might be someone who was always trying to save money by buying cheap, low-quality goods.

27. Hit the books

The idiom "hit the books" means to intensely study or work hard on a project. It is often used to describe a situation where someone is making a concerted effort to learn something or to prepare for an exam or test. The origins of this idiom are not clear, but it has been in use since the mid-20th century. It is likely that the phrase is related to similar phrases that use "hit" as a way of expressing the start of something, such as "hit the trail" or "hit the road." When someone "hits the books," they are usually studying, reading, or preparing for something with a long bout of determination and focus.

28. In the doghouse

In 1911's *Peter Pan*, written by J.M. Barrie, Mr. Darling punishes himself for allowing his children to be kidnapped by sleeping in the dog's kennel. While this would be a great origin story for the idiom, it's not feasible, as the word 'doghouse' was not used in Scotland, where Barrie was born, or in England, where he lived. The idiom first appeared in writing in 1926 in J.J. Finerty's *Criminalese*, a dictionary of criminal language. The phrase had been used prior but in a much more literal meaning. It became a famous saying in the United States in the 1930s. Today, the phrase is used more figuratively to describe someone who is in trouble or has been scolded or reprimanded. For instance, a spouse might be "in the doghouse" for failing to do any household duties or an employee might be reprimanded and "in the doghouse" at their job, meaning their boss is viewing them unfavorably.

29. Lots of moving parts

The idiom "lots of moving parts" is a phrase that describes the complexity of a system, process, or task that has multiple interrelated components that are constantly changing or interacting with each other. The origins of this idiom are rooted in the manufacturing or mechanical industry, where the concept of a machine with many moving parts that must work together seamlessly in order for the machine to function effectively, is a common one.

30. Cry wolf

The term "to cry wolf" is used to describe a situation where someone raises a false alarm or makes a false claim in order to gain attention or deceive others. The phrase originated from Aesop's ancient Greek fable "The Boy Who Cried Wolf" in which a boy repeatedly cries "wolf!" when there is no wolf, causing the villagers to ignore him when a real wolf comes. The phrase is also used to indicate that someone's credibility is in question because of their history of raising false alarms or making false claims. This phrase is a cautionary tale, it serves as a reminder to be honest and truthful in our communication and not to abuse people's trust.

Did You Know?

Shakespeare was born in Stratford-upon-Avon in 1564 to John Shakespeare, a successful glove-maker, and Mary Arden, the daughter of a well-to-do farmer. He was the third of eight children, and little is known about his childhood and education. However, it is believed that he received a good education and was well-versed in classical literature and the Bible.

In 1582, Shakespeare married Anne Hathaway, and they had three children together. In 1590, he moved to London to pursue a career in the theater, where he began working as an actor and writer. He quickly established himself as one of the most talented playwrights of his time, and his plays were performed at the Globe Theatre and the Blackfriars Theatre.

Throughout his career, Shakespeare wrote a wide variety of plays, including comedies, tragedies, and historical dramas. Some of his most famous works include *Macbeth*, *Hamlet*, *Romeo and Juliet*, *Othello*, and *The Tempest*. His plays are known for their memorable characters, complex plots, rich language and themes of love, jealousy, power, revenge, and the human condition.

In addition to his plays, Shakespeare also wrote a collection of sonnets, which are widely regarded as some of the greatest poems in the English language. The sonnets explore themes of love, beauty, and the passage of time and they remain popular and widely studied to this day.

Shakespeare's influence on the English language and literature is immense, and his plays and poems continue to be widely read, performed, and studied. He is often referred to as the "Bard of Avon" and is considered one of the greatest writers in the English language. He died in 1616 and was buried in Stratford-upon-Avon, England. Nevertheless, his legacy lives on, and his works continue to captivate audiences and inspire new generations of writers and artists.

31. Monday morning quarterback

The term "Monday morning quarterback" is a disapproving expression that refers to an individual who engages in the practice of criticizing the decisions and actions of others, particularly in relation to an event that has already occurred. This person offers their analysis and critiques from the perspective of 20/20 hindsight, without having been subject to the pressure or constraints of the situation. The phrase comes from American football, as most games are played on Sunday, and it is easy to critique a quarterback's decisions in the heat of the moment from the vantage point of the following day. The term was first coined by Barry Wood, the Harvard football team quarterback, during a speech in 1931.

32. Off the cuff

The phrase "off the cuff" is commonly used to describe a type of speaking or performance that is done without prior preparation. The idiom is thought to have originated in the world of jazz music, where musicians would often improvise solos on the spot, playing "off the cuff" rather than from a written score. The saying was popularized in the 1920s and 1930s when jazz music was at its peak in America. Nowadays, unrehearsed remarks or an impromptu moment caught on camera is said to be an "off the cuff" moment.

33. Wrap your head around something

The phrase "wrap your head around something" means coming to terms with something that is complex or challenging to understand. It is frequently used to describe the effort of making sense of an idea or concept that is difficult to grasp. This idiom made its first appearance in the *British boys'* magazine in the 1920s and has since gained widespread usage throughout the United States. It is synonymous with the phrase "getting one's head around," which was in common use prior to the emergence of "wrapping one's head around" as a popular idiom.

34. Go down in flames

The expression "to go down in flames" originated in the early 20th century during World War I and World War II, when airplanes were first utilized in warfare. The phrase comes from the imagery of an airplane crashing and catching fire, creating a fiery and explosive scene. This metaphor was initially used to describe the failure of a military mission, particularly when an aircraft was shot down in combat and crashed. However, as the term gained popularity, it started to be used more broadly to describe any dramatic and complete failure or collapse, in fields such as business, politics, and personal life.

35. Stitch up

The idiom "stitch up" is a British expression that means to deceive or betray someone, or to arrange things in a way that is dishonest or unfair. It is often used in a negative or critical way to imply that someone has been treated unfairly. It came about in the early 20th century from one of two sources. The first theory is that it originated in the world of criminal or underworld activity, where it was used to describe the act of framing someone or setting them up for a crime they did not commit. In this context, the "stitching" would refer to the act of deceit or betrayal, and the term "stitch up" would be used to describe someone who has been the victim of a dishonest or underhanded plot. The second theory is that the phrase comes from the idea of mending or repairing something that has been torn or damaged. In this case, the "stitching" would refer to the act of mending or fixing something, and the phrase "stitch up" would be used to describe someone who was able to repair a situation or solve a problem in a clever or resourceful way.

36. Haste makes waste

The idiom "haste makes waste" is a timeless piece of wisdom advising against rushing or acting hastily without careful consideration. When we use this phrase, we caution others (and ourselves) to slow down and think things through, as impulsive actions can lead to mistakes, inefficiency, and ultimately waste of time, effort, or resources. Its origins can be traced back to ancient proverbs and fables, like Aesop's *The Tortoise and the Hare*, where the moral of the story warns against overconfidence and rushing. Over time, this idiom has become a common saying in various cultures and languages, emphasizing the importance of prudence and deliberate decision-making. Today, we use it to remind ourselves to be patient, thorough, and mindful in our endeavors, ensuring better outcomes and avoiding unnecessary setbacks.

37. Like a cakewalk

The saying "like a cakewalk" means that something is very easy or effortless. The term is often used to describe a task or situation that requires little effort. The phrase is thought to have originated in the United States in the late 19th century and is often used colloquially in a lighthearted or humorous way. The word "cakewalk" originally referred to a type of dance popular in the late 19th century, characterized by its smooth and elegant style. It is thought that the phrase "like a cakewalk" evolved from this, with the idea being that something that is easy or effortless is similar to the graceful and easy-going nature of the cakewalk dance.

38. Run around in circles

The idiom "run around in circles" refers to a situation in which someone is making a lot of effort, but is not making any progress. It originated in the 19th century and likely developed from the literal practice of running in circles as a way to warm up or exercise. Today, it's often used to describe a situation in which someone is wasting their time or energy without achieving any results. The phrase can be applied to a variety of situations, such as trying to solve a problem or achieve a goal.

39. Get bent out of shape

"To get bent out of shape" means to become agitated or upset. It is often used to describe someone who becomes overly anxious or worked up about a situation that is not necessarily a big deal. Some sources suggest that the earliest meaning of the phrase was related to intoxication with alcohol, with "bent" being used to describe someone who was "drunk." As the decades progressed, the word "bent" was more commonly used to refer to someone getting upset. By the mid-1950s, the idiom was being used in its current form to describe someone who becomes agitated or upset due to stress or pressure.

40. Hunky dory

When everything's "hunky dory," everything is just fine. This expression first appeared in the United States in the 1860s when a Union soldier wrote to his family to tell them he was safe. Although it's unclear exactly where it originated, the word "hunk" was slang for a "safe place." The "dory" could be attributed to wordplay to give the term a singsong tone. Another explanation for the term was that it was brought back by sailors who had traveled to Japan in the 1850s to engage in trade. Honcho Dori Street in Yokohama was a popular destination for sailors; its streets were lined with establishments where sailors could enjoy themselves. It's said that the sailors, not familiar with the Japanese language, nicknamed the road Hunky-Dory and associated it with a place where everything was just fine.

Did You Know?

Confucius was a Chinese philosopher and teacher who lived in the Eastern Zhou period (5th century BC) in ancient China. He is one of the most influential figures in Chinese history and his teachings and ideas have had a profound impact on Chinese culture, politics, and philosophy.

Confucius was born in 551 BC in Qufu, Shandong province in China. He was born into a poor family, but he was highly intelligent and showed a keen interest in learning from a young age. He studied a wide variety of subjects, including literature, music, history, and the arts, and he later became a teacher, sharing his knowledge and wisdom with others.

Confucius believed in the importance of education and personal development. He believed that individuals could achieve moral and ethical excellence through self-discipline and the pursuit of knowledge. He also believed in the importance of family values, such as filial piety, and he encouraged people to cultivate good relationships with others through honesty, fairness, and respect.

Confucius' teachings were recorded by his disciples in a collection of texts known as the *Analects*. The *Analects* contain a wide range of Confucius' ideas, including his thoughts on education, ethics, and politics, and they remain an important source of Chinese philosophy to this day.

Confucius' impact on Chinese culture and history is immense, and his teachings continue to be widely studied and revered. He is the founder of Confucianism, one of the major philosophical schools of ancient China, and his ideas have influenced a wide variety of fields, including politics, education, and ethics. Confucius' legacy lives on, and he remains one of the most important figures in Chinese history and culture.

41. Rat race

The term "rat race" originated from the practice of placing rats in circular cages and observing them as they run in a seemingly endless pursuit for a reward. In the real world, the phrase is used to describe the competitive and hectic nature of modern urban life, especially in the context of work and career. The expression implies that people are caught up in a meaningless, endless, and frantic pursuit of success and material wealth, akin to rats running in a maze in search of a reward. The rats would spend more energy than the reward is worth in the process, in a futile and mad competition.

42. Knock yourself out

The phrase "knock yourself out" is a colloquial expression that means "go ahead" or "do what you want," often used to give someone permission or encouragement. It can also be used to express sarcasm or irony, especially when trying to do something that is unnecessary. The term originated in the 20th century from the practice of boxers knocking themselves out in the ring. It can also be used in the sense of someone doing an activity to the point of exhaustion, as in knocking oneself out trying to do something.

43. Move heaven and earth

The idiom "move heaven and earth" conveys the idea of making a great effort or going to great lengths to accomplish something. The term probably came into use in the 1700s. Despite its uncertain origin, there are a few theories as to where it may have originated from. One theory is that the it's related to Archimedes' statement "Give me a lever long enough and a fulcrum on which to place it, and I shall move the world." However, it is worth noting that Archimedes lived in the 200s BC and the idiom did not come into use until two thousand years later. Another theory attributes the idiom to a passage in the Bible, Haggai 2:6: "… I will shake the heavens, and the earth, and the sea, and the dry land…" However, the word "move" is not an accurate synonym of the word "shake" in this context. Nowadays, when people say they will "move heaven and earth," it is often a statement that implies that the person won't give up and use whatever strength and resources they have to reach a goal.

44. The early bird catches the worm

"The early bird catches the worm" is a timeless idiom conveying the idea that those who act promptly and seize opportunities have an advantage. We use this expression to encourage proactive behavior and prompt action. Its origins can be traced back to the 17th century, with variations appearing in writings by John Ray and William Camden. Its first written form was in Ray's collection of English proverbs in 1670. Over time, the phrase evolved to emphasize the significance of being proactive and diligent to achieve success. Today, we use it to motivate ourselves and others to be proactive, seize opportunities, and stay ahead in various endeavors, from education and business to personal growth.

45. Nip in the bud

The idiom "nip in the bud" describes the act of preventing something from developing or becoming a bigger problem by dealing with it at an early stage. The phrase is often used in the context of stopping a conflict or issue before it has a chance to grow or become more serious. The origin of the expression is derived from gardening, where it is common practice to cut off the buds of a plant before they have a chance to develop into flowers or fruits, in order to prevent the plant from wasting energy on unnecessary growth.

46. A stone's throw

The idiom "a stone's throw" is used to indicate that something is situated very close to another location. The phrase suggests that the distance between two places is so short that a stone could be thrown from one place to the other. The origins of this expression can be traced back to ancient times, when stones were commonly used as a weapon, and were thrown by hand or with a sling. Early English versions of the Bible also refer to "a stone's cast" with the same meaning, as in Luke 22:41, Wycliffe's Bible, 1526: "he gat himself from them, about a stone's cast."

47. Close shave

The phrase "close shave" means to narrowly avoid danger or a difficult situation. The origins of the phrase can be traced back to the act of shaving, specifically the use of a straight razor, which required skill and precision to avoid cutting oneself. The words "a close shave" were first recorded in 1825 and are considered an Americanism. In modern times, you could use the term "a close call" and "a close shave" interchangeably.

48. Tongue-in-cheek

The idiom "tongue-in-cheek" is used like an adjective to describe a statement or remark that is not meant to be taken seriously, often being made in a humorous or playful way. One theory of its origin is that it comes from sailing culture, referring to the practice of sailors putting their tongue in the cheek to indicate to their fellow sailors that they are joking or not to take their statement seriously. The first recorded use of the phrase in literature is from Scottish novelist Sir Walter Scott's 1828 book *The Fair Maid of Perth*, where the gesture of tongue-in-cheek is described, but it's not clear if it was intended to mean "not really." However, the use of the phrase in its modern sense is more clearly seen in a later citation by English poet Richard Barham in his 1845 collection of stories and poems *The Ingoldsby Legends* where the term is used to indicate sarcasm and irony. In this day and age, people might post "tongue-in-cheek" comments online or friends could make "tongue-in-cheek" remarks to each other while everyone knows what is being said isn't to be take seriously.

49. Spitting image

The term "spitting image" is used to describe someone who closely resembles another person, usually a parent or ancestor. The phrase became popular in the late 19th century, but the concept and expression was in circulation as early as 1689, when George Farquhar used it in his play *Love and a Bottle*: "Poor child! He's as like his own dada as if he were spit out of his mouth."

50. Hump day

The term "hump day" refers to the middle of the workweek, specifically Wednesday for most folks, which is often considered the "hump" to get over in order to reach the end of the week and the weekend. The phrase is often used in a lighthearted and humorous manner to help motivate people to push through the middle of the week. The term was popular in the 1980s but gained even more traction in 2013, when GEICO (an insurance company) created a popular commercial featuring a camel named "Cameron the Camel" strolling around an office and asking coworkers what day it was. The commercial ended with the punchline, "It's hump day!" After the commercial aired, the phrase became widely used and popularized as a way to refer to Wednesday.

Did You Know?

Socrates was a classical Greek philosopher and is considered the founder of Western philosophy. He lived in Athens, Greece from 470-399 BC and is best known for his method of inquiry, known as the Socratic method, which involves asking questions to encourage critical thinking and problem solving. Socrates left no written works and much of what we know about him comes from the writings of his students, Plato and Xenophon.

Socrates was born in Athens to a family of modest means. He served as a hoplite (a type of infantryman) in the Athenian army during the Peloponnesian War, and it is said that he performed with bravery and distinction. After the war, Socrates turned to philosophy, and he spent the rest of his life engaging in philosophical dialogues and discussions with the people of Athens.

Socrates was a man of great integrity and courage. He was known for his unwavering commitment to the pursuit of wisdom and the importance of self-reflection. He believed that the only true wisdom was the knowledge of one's own ignorance and that it was only through questioning and examining one's own beliefs that true wisdom could be achieved. This approach to philosophy became known as the Socratic method, and it has had a profound impact on Western thought and culture.

One of the most famous episodes in the life of Socrates is his trial and execution. He was charged with corrupting the youth of Athens and impiety, and he was sentenced to death by drinking hemlock. Socrates was given the opportunity to escape, but he refused, stating that he would not betray his principles for the sake of his own life. His death is considered a turning point in Western thought and has become a symbol of the struggle for intellectual freedom and the pursuit of wisdom.

51. See eye to eye

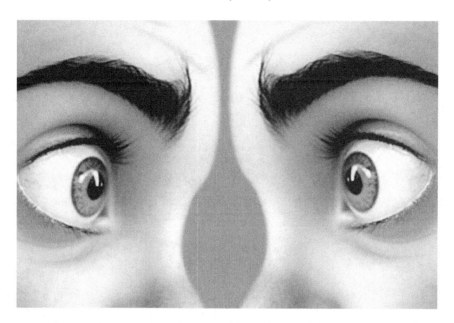

To "see eye to eye" is an idiom that indicates that two or more people are in agreement or understanding on a particular matter. The origins of this phrase date back to the 16th century, where it was used to describe a situation where people were able to look each other in the eyes as a way of expressing mutual understanding. The phrase, however, was taken from a biblical passage, Isaiah chapter 52 verse 8 of the King James Version: "…for they shall see eye to eye, when the Lord shall bring again Zion." In this passage, the expression see eye to eye means to meet face-to-face, or in person.

52. A piece of the pie

"A piece of the pie" is a flavorful idiom that signifies a share or portion of something desirable, often related to wealth, success, or benefits. We use this expression when talking about gaining a fair portion of resources or opportunities in a particular venture or endeavor. Its origins can be traced to the early 1900s in America, where "pie" symbolized prosperity and abundance. Although the exact first use in writing is unclear, the idiom gained popularity during the mid-20th century. Over time, its meaning expanded beyond financial matters, representing equitable distribution or fair participation in various contexts, including business deals, projects, and even family affairs. Today, we use it playfully and metaphorically, emphasizing the importance of receiving a fair share and partaking in the rewards of success.

53. Rome wasn't built in a day

The idiom "Rome wasn't built in a day" serves as a gentle reminder that significant achievements take time and cannot be rushed. We use it to encourage patience and perseverance when tackling ambitious projects or pursuing long-term goals. The saying's origins can be traced back to the 12th-century French phrase "Rome ne fut pas faite toute en un jour" and has since been adapted and translated across languages. While the exact first use in writing is unclear, its essence remains consistent: complex undertakings, like building a great city or achieving remarkable success, require careful planning, dedication, and sustained effort over time. The idiom has evolved into a universal expression, applicable in various contexts, from personal development to business ventures. In modern times, we use the phrase to remind ourselves and others that progress may be gradual, but with perseverance and determination, extraordinary accomplishments can be achieved.

54. Two heads are better than one

The expression "two heads are better than one" conveys the idea that collaborating with others can lead to better solutions and ideas than working alone. We use it to emphasize the value of teamwork, shared knowledge, and diverse perspectives in problem-solving or decision-making situations. Its origins can be traced back to a 1546 English proverb, "Two heads are better than one, especially if one is a sheep." Over time, the phrase evolved to its current form, reflecting the belief that pooling intelligence and skills enhances creativity and problem-solving capabilities. In today's fast-paced and interconnected world, we apply the idiom in various contexts, such as brainstorming sessions, group projects, or team discussions, where the collaboration of multiple individuals can lead to innovative and well-rounded outcomes.

55. High and mighty

The expression "high and mighty" is often used to describe someone who acts arrogant and superior, exhibiting a sense of self-importance and a tendency to look down on others. This person may treat others with disdain or contempt as if they believe themselves to be "higher" and "mightier" in some way. The phrase has a long history, with one of the earliest recorded uses dating back to the letter written in 1420 by Robert Waterton to King Henry V. In the letter, King Henry is referred to as a "right excellent high and right mighty Prince and most dreaded sovereign Lord." This suggests that the phrase has been used for centuries to describe those who hold themselves in high regard and believe to be superior to others. In modern times, the idiom "high and mighty" is often used to describe individuals who exhibit arrogant or pretentious behavior, which is generally considered a negative trait.

56. A dime a dozen

The idiom "a dime a dozen" refers to something that is abundant and ubiquitous, thus considered inexpensive or of little value. The phrase originates from the fact that a dime is a unit of US currency that is worth ten cents. The dime coin was first minted in 1796, and in the 1800s, many goods, such as eggs or apples, were advertised as costing a dime a dozen in the United States, indicating they were being sold at good value for the money. However, over time, the meaning of the phrase evolved to indicate the opposite, referring to something that is nearly worthless due to its commonness and easy availability. The first recorded use of the expression in this context was in 1930 and continues to be used in the same way today.

57. Yellow

The idiom "yellow" means to be cowardly or lacking in courage. It originated in the early 20th century and comes from the idea of the color yellow being associated with cowardice or treachery. There are a few different theories about how the color yellow came to be associated with cowardice. One theory is that it originated in the military, where soldiers who were considered to be brave or courageous would wear red or blue uniforms, while those who were considered to be less brave or cowardly would wear yellow. Another theory is that the association may have come from the way that some animals, such as chickens, are known to turn yellow when they are frightened or stressed. Regardless of its origins, the word "yellow" is now widely used in English in a derogatory or mocking way to imply that someone is afraid or lacks the courage to do something.

58. Sell like hot cakes

The idiom "sell like hot cakes" is used to describe a situation where something is in high demand and is selling quickly. It likely originated from the popularity of hot cakes as a breakfast food in the United States in the 19th and early 20th centuries. In this context, the phrase "sell like hot cakes" referred to the ease with which hot cakes were sold due to their popularity. The phrase is now used more broadly to refer to any situation where a product or service is highly sought-after and selling at a fast pace. It can be used to describe a variety of items, such as products, services, and tickets for events.

59. The jig is up

The phrase "the jig is up" is used to express that a deception or a secret has been discovered, and that the person responsible is likely to be caught or held accountable. The phrase originated in the late 19th century, however the exact etymology is uncertain. One theory suggests that it comes from the word "jig" which was a slang term for a deception or a trick, and that when the "jig is up," the trick has been discovered. Another theory is that it comes from the dance, "jig," where the music would stop and the dancers would be caught if they were doing something wrong.

60. Shed light on

The idiomatic expression "to shed light on" means to provide information or understanding about something, to make something clear, or to reveal something that was previously unknown or difficult to understand. The origins of the phrase can be traced back to the everyday act of lighting a room or space with a candle or fire. The act of illuminating a space was known as "shedding light" in Europe, thus the term came to be used to describe the clearing of doubts or the making of a complicated situation clearer.

Did You Know?

Aesop was a legendary ancient Greek storyteller who lived between 620-560 BC. Although not much is known about his life, his tales have been popular and widely read for centuries. Aesop's fables are a collection of stories, each with a moral lesson, and are meant to educate and entertain the audience. The tales feature animals with human-like characteristics and often reflect on universal truths and wisdom.

The exact origins of Aesop's fables are not known and the storyteller himself is shrouded in mystery. Some historical accounts suggest that he was born a slave in Thrace and later freed by his master, while others claim that he was born free in Phrygia. Regardless of his origins, Aesop became famous for his wit, wisdom, and storytelling skills, as he traveled throughout Greece to tell his tales.

Aesop's fables have been passed down from generation to generation and have been translated into many languages. The tales are known for their simple, yet profound, messages and have been used as a means of teaching moral values to children and adults alike. Some of the most famous fables include "The Ant and the Grasshopper," "The Tortoise and the Hare," and "The Boy Who Cried Wolf."

61. Gloves are off

The idiom "the gloves are off" connotes the removal of constraints or inhibitions and the readiness to engage in a fight (either physically or figuratively). The origins of this phrase are likely rooted in the practice of removing gloves before engaging in a physical fight. It is commonly associated with boxing gloves and the increased brutality and damage that would occur in a match without them. However, an earlier variant of the idiom, "to handle someone without gloves," was in use since the early 1800s and shared a similar meaning of dealing with someone in a rough and uncompromising way. Since boxing with gloves was uncommon until the late 1800s, it appears that the idiom does not specifically derive from boxing but rather from the allusion to men taking their gloves off to prepare for a serious and possibly violent confrontation. In more polite society, a person might say "the gloves are coming off" before they tackle a big project at work or a tough task that requires a lot of effort.

62. Land of milk and honey

The "land of milk and honey" is a colloquial expression that means a place of abundance and prosperity, often used to describe a utopia or paradise. The phrase is often used in a metaphorical sense to describe a place where everything is perfect and everything is available in abundance. It originates from the Hebrew Bible, specifically in the book of Exodus, where God promised the Israelites that he would lead them to a land flowing with milk and honey: "And I am come down to deliver them out of the hand of the Egyptians, and to bring them up out of that land unto a good land and a large, unto a land flowing with milk and honey..." The expression is also found in the book of Numbers and Leviticus.

63. Bone to pick

The idiom "bone to pick" means to have a disagreement or issue to resolve. The phrase is often used as "to have a bone to pick with (someone)," which means to have a specific issue or problem that needs to be addressed with that person. Most sources state that this expression comes from a dog trying to pick off the meat from a bone, and one connotation of this idiom is trying to solve a difficult, time-consuming problem. This is likely related to the fact that dogs often gnaw on a bone for very long periods of time, even when most of the meat is gone. This type of usage dates back to the 1500s. The other more common connotation of the phrase is to try to settle a dispute with someone. This usage goes back to the 1800s. Alternatively, it might come from the idea of two dogs fighting over a bone.

64. By the skin of your teeth

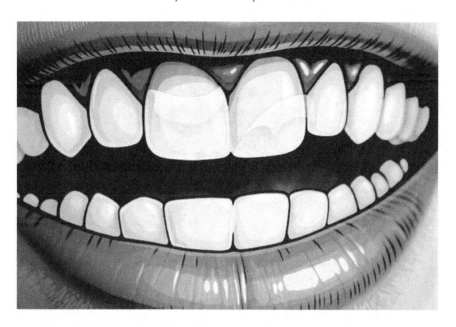

The idiom "by the skin of your teeth" refers to a situation in which someone barely succeeds or avoids something, often by a very narrow margin or with great difficulty. It originated in the 16th century and is likely derived from the Biblical phrase "delivered by the skin of their teeth," which appears in *The Book of Job*. Today, the term is used to convey a sense of narrow escape or close call.

65. Gray area

The term "gray area" refers to a situation or issue that is not clearly defined or that falls between two clearly defined categories or extremes. It is often used to describe something that is ambiguous or open to interpretation, or that is not easily classified as right or wrong. The origin of the phrase "gray area" is not entirely clear, but it is thought to have originated in the 20th century. One theory is that it originated from the use of the color gray to represent neutrality or ambiguity. Another theory is that the phrase originated in the field of psychology, where it was used to describe a range of behaviors or experiences that fall between normal and abnormal. In this context, the "gray area" would refer to the range of behaviors or experiences that are not clearly defined as normal or abnormal, but that fall somewhere in between.

66. You can't have your cake and eat it too

The idiom "you can't have your cake and eat it too" is a well-known English expression that conveys the idea that one cannot have or enjoy all the benefits of a situation without having to accept the drawbacks or consequences as well. It is often used to indicate that one must make a choice between two mutually exclusive options. The origins of this idiom can be traced back to the early 1600s, with the earliest known written record of the phrase appearing in a poem by John Heywood in 1546. The same sentiment of the necessity of making a choice may be found in other idioms from different cultures, such as the Albanian proverb that says "you cannot take a swim and not get wet" or the German saying that states "you cannot dance at two weddings at the same time," "you can't make an omelette without breaking eggs" in French, and "you can't have the fruit and the seed" in Spanish. In British English, the last word is often omitted from the proverb, as in "you can't have your cake and eat it."

67. Leave no stone unturned

The idiom "leave no stone unturned" means to make a thorough and exhaustive effort to achieve a goal or solve a problem. It suggests that the person or group in question is determined, persistent, and willing to explore every possible option or avenue to achieve their desired outcome. The story of its origin dates back to a Greek legend. A general of Xerxes named Mardonius was believed to have buried treasure near his tent. In 447 BC, when Mardonius was defeated at the battle of Plataea, Polycrates of Thebes began searching for the treasure to no avail. He consulted the Oracle of Delphi, who advised him to look under every stone. When the medieval scholar Erasmus translated the story into Latin, he quoted the Oracle as saying, "leave no stone unturned." Erasmus' work was translated into English in the 1500s, and the expression has been used since then.

68. Cooking the books

"Cooking the books" is an expression that refers to the act of falsifying or manipulating financial records or accounts in order to deceive or mislead others. It usually refers to accounting fraud, where companies falsify their financial statements to make them appear more profitable or financially stable than they really are. This can be done in various ways, such as by understating expenses, overstating revenues, or creating false entries in the financial records. This type of fraud can be committed by individuals within a company, and it can have serious consequences for investors, employees, and the company as a whole. The phrase has been used since the 17th century, as evidenced by the Earl of Strafford in his *Letters and Dispatches* from 1636, where he wrote, "The proof was once clear, however they have cook'd it since."

69. Jam on the brakes

To "jam on the brakes" means to make a sudden, forceful stop, usually while driving a vehicle. It is often used to describe a sudden, unexpected stop or a stop made in an emergency situation. The origin of this idiom is thought to be related to the physical act of pressing down on the brake pedal of a vehicle in order to bring it to a stop. The metaphor suggests that one is making a sudden and forceful stop, much like one might press down hard on the brake pedal to bring a vehicle to a rapid stop. The earliest written use of this phrase dates back to the early 20th century. It appears in a book called *The Motor Boys on the Pacific* by Clarence Young, which was published in 1906. The book includes the line, "I just jammed on the brakes and stopped." In casual conversation, however, you could say to someone "let's jam on the breaks," meaning that they are talking too much and you want them to stop or they are going on and on about something that is making you uncomfortable and you need a break.

70. Needle in a haystack

The famous idiom "needle in a haystack" is a powerful metaphor that is used to describe an elusive or difficult-to-find object, situation, or information. It often conveys the idea that something is so insignificant or small in comparison to the larger surrounding area that it becomes almost impossible to locate. The origins of this phrase can be traced back to the practice of farming, where needles, which were handcrafted and made of materials that blended in with hay, were difficult to locate within a haystack. Another idiom with the word needle is "move the needle" which is a metaphor that describes a significant improvement or change in a situation or performance.

Did You Know?

- The word "quarantine" comes from the Italian "quaranta giorni," which means "forty days." The term originally described the practice of isolating ships that arrived in port for forty days to prevent the spread of infectious diseases.
- The word "algebra" comes from the Arabic "al-jabr," which means "the reunion of broken parts." It was used by the mathematician Muhammad ibn Musa al-Khwarizmi to describe a system for solving equations.
- The word "sarcasm" comes from the Greek "sarkasmos," which means "to tear flesh, bite the lip in rage, sneer." It originally referred to a sharp, bitter, or cutting remark.
- The word "quark" comes from the German "quark," which means "curd." It was coined by the physicist Murray Gell-Mann to describe a type of subatomic particle.

71. To see red

The expression "to see red" is used to describe a feeling of extreme anger or rage. It originated in the early 20th century and is derived from the association of the color red with anger and violence. When someone is "seeing red," they are experiencing a strong emotional response characterized by intense anger and a desire to lash out. The phrase is often used to describe someone who is visibly upset and angry, and may be accompanied by physical signs of rage such as clenched fists, reddened face, and raised voice. It is typically used in a metaphorical sense and does not mean that someone is literally seeing the color red.

72. Tip of the iceberg

The "tip of the iceberg" refers to a small part of a larger problem or situation that is visible or apparent, but the vast majority remains hidden. It is used to convey the idea that what is visible is only a small part of a much larger issue. The idiom is often used in a negative context, to describe a situation where the true extent of a problem or issue is not immediately obvious. The origin of the phrase comes from the literal appearance of icebergs, which are large chunks of ice floating in the ocean. Only the top of the iceberg is visible above the waterline, while the vast majority of the iceberg remains hidden underwater. The first recorded use of the phrase in print is from a 1912 article in the *New York Times*, describing the sinking of the ocean liner RMS Titanic, which struck an iceberg and sank.

73. Draw a line in the sand

The idiomatic expression "draw a line in the sand" is a colloquial way of establishing a clear and decisive boundary or a point of no return. The origins of this phrase can be traced back to a number of historical references, such as in the Bible, where it refers to Jesus' writing in the sand, in the Ramayana where a circle was drawn around someone for protection, and in Roman history where the phrase was used to indicate a clear stance on a political issue. One of the most notable historical references is from 168 BC, when a Roman Consul named Gaius Popillius Laenas drew a circular line in the sand around King Antiochus IV of the Seleucid Empire, then said, "Before you cross this circle I want you to give me a reply for the Roman Senate" – implying that Rome would declare war if the King stepped out of the circle without committing to leave Egypt immediately. Weighing his options, Antiochus wisely decided to withdraw. Only then did Popillius agree to shake hands with him. In modern times, a person might "draw a line in the sand" in a relationship to unambiguously let the other person know what behaviors or actions they will not tolerate.

74. The final straw

The "the final straw" is derived from the phrase "the last straw that broke the camel's back." It refers to a situation where one last event or action causes a person to reach their breaking point and respond with a strong reaction, usually anger or frustration. It is often used in a situation where someone has tolerated a negative behavior for a long time, but one final event pushes them over the edge. The term "the last feather breaks the horse's back" is an earlier version of this idiom, dating back to the 1800s. The origin of the phrase comes from the old practice of loading heavy loads on the back of a camel or a donkey. The earliest example of the idiom can be found in *The Edinburgh Advertiser*, from May 1816, where the phrase is used in the context of a rich man who used camels to transport his straw. He would load as much straw as he could on them in order to get the most out of the animals. One day he proceeded to load one last piece of straw onto the camel's back and the camel collapsed.

75. Doesn't cut the mustard

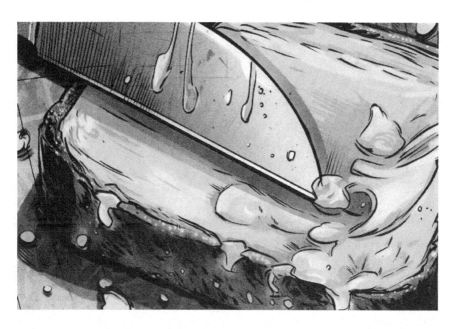

The odd idiom "doesn't cut the mustard" is used to convey that something or someone is not of sufficient quality or fails to meet the required standard. It implies that the person or thing being referred to is inadequate or unsatisfactory. The phrase is believed to have originated from the farming practice of cutting mustard, which was one of the main crops in East Anglia in Britain. Mustard was traditionally cut by hand with scythes, similar to corn. As the crop could grow up to six feet high, it required extremely sharp tools. When the tools were not sharp enough, they "would not cut the mustard" resulting in the work being more difficult and less efficient.

76. From the bottom of one's heart

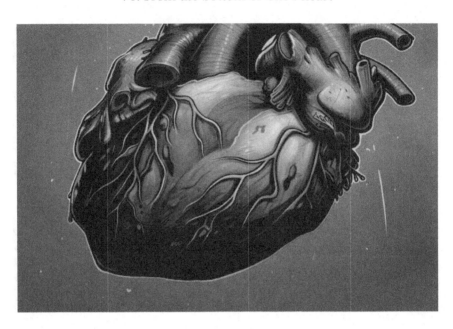

"From the bottom of one's heart" is an idiomatic expression that indicates that something is said or done with genuine sincerity and emotion. One theory about its origins is that it dates back to ancient Greece when the philosopher Archimedes mistakenly believed that the heart was responsible for thinking and feeling, while the brain pumped blood. According to this theory, this belief may have led to the idea that when something is said or done "from the bottom of one's heart," it is coming from a place of deep, genuine feeling.

77. Off the table

The idiom "off the table" is used to indicate that something is no longer being considered or is not an option anymore. It is often used in a negotiation or decision-making context to indicate that a particular proposal, idea, or option has been rejected or is no longer open for discussion. The phrase suggests that the item in question has been physically removed from the table, signifying that it is no longer under consideration. The origins of this idiom come from a literal meaning of taking something off a table so that the parties making a deal can't bicker over it further.

78. Round the bend

The expression "round the bend" means to be crazy or mentally unbalanced. It is often used to describe someone who is behaving in an irrational or unpredictable way, or who is showing signs of mental instability. The origin of this idiom is not clear, but it is thought to be related to the idea of going around a bend or curve in a road. The metaphor suggests that one is going off in an unexpected or unusual direction, much like a road might curve or bend unexpectedly. An early written use of this phrase dates back to the early 20th century. It appears in a book called *The Delectable Duchy* by Arthur Thomas Quiller-Couch, which was published in 1913. The book includes the line, "He had a good heart, and a clear head; but he was round the bend a little, as the saying is."

79. You reap what you sow

The phrase "you reap what you sow" serves as a reminder that our actions have consequences, and we will face the results of our choices, whether positive or negative. We use it to underscore the principle of cause and effect, highlighting the importance of being mindful of our deeds and decisions. The expression has biblical origins and can be found in Galatians 6:7, "Do not be deceived: God cannot be mocked. A man reaps what he sows." Over time, the idiom has transcended its religious roots and become a widely recognized proverb across cultures, emphasizing personal responsibility and accountability for our actions. Today, we use it as a cautionary tale to encourage thoughtful and ethical behavior, understanding that the outcomes we experience in life are a direct result of the choices we make.

80. Barrel of laughs

The expression "a barrel of laughs" means that something or someone is very amusing or entertaining. It is often said in a lighthearted or playful manner, indicating that the speaker finds the person or thing to be a source of joy or enjoyment. It is thought to have originated in the United States in the early 20th century and has been in widespread use since then. The phrase likely comes from the concept of a "barrel of monkeys," a toy consisting of small, plastic monkeys that are strung together and can be manipulated to form different shapes or configurations. The toy is known for being entertaining, particularly for children. It is likely that the phrase "a barrel of laughs" was originally used to describe something that was similarly amusing.

Did You Know?

January is the first month of the year in our modern calendar. It is derived from the Latin "Januarius," which is named after the Roman god Janus, who was the god of beginnings and endings.

February is derived from the Latin "Februarius," which is named after the festival of Februa, a purification ritual that was held during the month.

March is derived from the Latin "Martius," which is named after the Roman god Mars, who was the god of war.

April is derived from the Latin "Aprilis," which is probably derived from the Greek word "apros," meaning "to open," as this was the time of year when plants and flowers began to open and bloom.

May is derived from the Latin "Maius," which is named after the Roman goddess Maia, who was the mother of Mercury, the messenger of the gods.

June is derived from the Latin "Junius," which is named after the Roman goddess Juno, who was the wife of Jupiter, the king of the gods.

81. Off the hook

The expression "off the hook" means to be relieved or freed from a difficult situation, responsibility, or obligation. We use it when someone is no longer accountable for something they were previously expected to do or when they escape a potential consequence. The origins of this idiom are believed to stem from fishing, where "off the hook" literally refers to a fish escaping from the fishing line, thus avoiding capture. The phrase might have been used informally in speech for a long time, but its first documented appearance in writing is unclear. Over time, its meaning has evolved to include various contexts, such as being cleared of blame or no longer having to deal with an undesirable situation. Today we often use it in everyday conversations to express relief or a sense of freedom from a particular responsibility or trouble.

82. Preaching to the choir

The idiom "preaching to the choir" is a variation of the earlier phrase "preaching to the converted." The concept of preaching to those already in agreement with a particular belief or viewpoint can be traced back to an 1857 article in *The Times* which stated, "It is an old saying that to preach to the converted is a useless office, and I may add that to preach to the unconvertible is a thankless office." The modern iteration of the phrase, "preaching to the choir," is of American origin. The first recorded use of the phrase in this format can be found in 1973, in *The Lima News* in Ohio, where it was used to describe a minister preaching to regular church attendees rather than those in need of the message.

83. More bang for one's buck

The origin of the idiom "more bang for one's buck" can be traced back to the early 20th century, when "bang" was used as slang to refer to excitement or thrill. It is believed that the phrase was first used in the context of entertainment, such as carnivals or circuses, where one would want to get the most excitement or thrills for their money. The phrase then gained popularity during World War II, as the US military sought to make the most out of their limited resources. The military needed to maximize the effectiveness of their weapons and equipment and thus the phrase "more bang for one's buck" was used to refer to getting the most firepower for the amount of money or resources invested. The phrase then was adopted by civilians and has been used in various contexts such as business, marketing and everyday life. It is used to describe a product, service, or investment that offers a lot of features or benefits for a relatively low cost.

84. A win-win situation

The phrase "a win-win situation" refers to a scenario in which all parties benefit or are satisfied with the outcome. The metaphor suggests that all parties involved are able to "win," or achieve their goals. This isn't often the case in politics or business, but when both sides come out happy and satisfied that they got what they wanted it is a "win-win." The earliest written use of this phrase dates back to the late 20th century and it appears in a book called *The Psychology of Persuasion* by Robert B. Cialdini, which was published in 1984. The book includes the line, "In a win-win situation, everyone involved benefits."

85. On sixes and sevens

The idiom "on sixes and sevens" is used to describe a state of confusion or disorder. It can refer to a scene of overall chaos, or to describe a group of people who are unable to agree or make a decision. There are a few theories about the origin of this idiom. The first theory is that it originated in the 1300s. At that time, the phrase was "on six and seven," and it referred to a dice game in which a roll of six or seven meant that a player was risking their entire fortune. The second theory suggests that it may have originated in medieval England, where it was used to describe a state of disarray or confusion. The third theory is that it originated in ancient Rome, where the number six was considered unlucky and the number seven was lucky. The earliest written use of the phrase "on sixes and sevens" appears in a book called *The Proverbs, Epigrams, and Miscellanies* by John Heywood, which was published in 1562. The book includes the line, "As a man on six and seven, that knoweth not whether he be on horseback or on foot."

86. Fool's gold

The term "fool's gold" describes something that appears valuable, but is actually worthless. The phrase originated in the 19th century from the mining industry, where iron pyrite, a mineral that closely resembles gold, was often mistaken for the real thing by inexperienced prospectors. The name "fool's gold" was given to this mineral due to the fact that it often led to disappointment for those who mistook it for the real thing. Nowadays, an ill-advised investment, a sill technologic pursuit, or a misleading piece of advice could all be "fool's gold."

87. Batten down the hatches

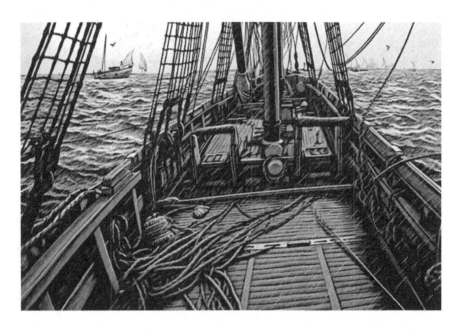

The idiom "batten down the hatches" has its roots in the nautical world of medieval times, when ship travel was a common mode of transportation to new territories. The English used navies and ships to establish colonies around the world. The term literally refers to the practice of covering the openings on the deck of a ship, known as hatches, with tarpaulin and wooden strips called battens, in order to prevent water from entering the ship during bad weather. The sailors would refer to this activity as "battening down." The phrase has been in use since at least 1769, with references to it in *An Universal Dictionary of the Marine* by William Falconer. Despite variations in spelling of the word "batten" such as "battern" and "baton," the meaning of the phrase has remained the same. In modern times, you could "batten down the hatches" by boarding up or protecting your home or property before a storm, or the phrase can be used in a more figurative sense to prepare oneself for a coming struggle or confrontation.

88. Foul play

"Foul play" refers to dishonest or malicious actions, typically in the context of sports or games. It is thought to have originated in the sport of cricket, where it was used to describe actions that violated the rules of the game. In modern usage, the term is used more broadly to describe any situation where someone has acted dishonestly in order to gain an advantage. It's colloquially used in reference to criminal investigations, where it may be suggested that a crime was committed in a premeditated manner. The phrase is often used as a warning or cautionary message, indicating that someone or something may be acting in a way that is not above board or that may be harmful to others.

89. Something has legs

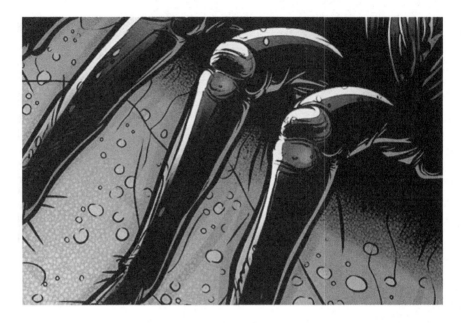

To say that "something has legs" indicates that an idea or a situation has the potential to grow or develop. The phrase originated in the early 20th century, and is based on the imagery of something that can carry itself forward on its legs. It's often used to describe an idea or a situation that has the potential to be successful or have a long-term impact.

90. Bend over backwards

If you "bend over backwards" you are making a very strong or extreme effort to do something, often in order to help or accommodate someone else. This idiom originated in the United States in the 20th century and comes from the literal act of bending over backwards, which is a very difficult and strenuous physical position to maintain. The phrase suggests that the person in question is making an immense effort to accomplish something, often to the point of straining themselves or going to great lengths to achieve their goal. Today, the idiom is frequently used in a positive or complimentary way, implying that a person is going above and beyond to assist others.

Did You Know?

July is derived from the Latin "Julius," which is named after Julius Caesar, the Roman general and statesman.

August is derived from the Latin "Augustus," which is named after Augustus Caesar, the first Roman emperor.

September is derived from the Latin "September," which means "seventh" in Latin, as it was originally the seventh month of the Roman calendar.

October is derived from the Latin "October," which means "eighth" in Latin, as it was originally the eighth month of the Roman calendar.

November is derived from the Latin "November," which means "ninth" in Latin, as it was originally the ninth month of the Roman calendar.

December is derived from the Latin "December," which means "tenth" in Latin, as it was originally the tenth month of the Roman calendar.

91. Diamond in the rough

The phrase "diamond in the rough" refers to someone or something that has potential or value, but is not yet fully developed or polished. The origin of the phrase comes from the process of diamond mining, where a diamond in its natural state, before it is cut and polished, is often referred to as a "rough diamond." This term was used as early as the 1600s and it first appeared in print in John Fletcher's 1624 play *A Wife for a Month*, where it is written, "She is very honest, and will be as hard to cut as a rough diamond." One fun fact about diamonds is that they are made up of pure carbon, the same element that makes up graphite in pencils. However, the unique way in which the carbon atoms are arranged in a diamond gives it its exceptional strength and durability, as well as its iconic sparkle and brilliance. Nowadays, we might say that a person with budding talent but is yet unknown or a product that hasn't taken off yet are "diamonds in the rough."

92. In for a penny in for a pound

The idiom "in for a penny, in for a pound" refers to a situation in which someone decides to fully commit to a task or venture, even if it requires a significant amount of time, effort, or resources. It originated in the 17th century and is derived from the phrase "all in for a penny, all in for a pound," which was used to describe the act of gambling with a small amount of money in the hope of winning a larger amount. Today the expression is often used to convey a sense of determination or commitment.

93. Be in a tight corner

To "be in a tight corner" means to be in a difficult situation. It often describes a circumstance in which someone is facing challenges or problems that are hard to overcome. There are two different theories about the origins of this phrase. The first is that it comes from the idea of being trapped or cornered in a physical sense, such as being trapped in a small space or against a wall, suggesting that the idiom originally referred to the feeling of being physically trapped or confined. The second is related to the expression "in a bind," which means to be in a difficult or challenging situation, suggesting that the idiom originally referred to the idea of being caught or trapped in a difficult situation that is hard to escape from.

94. Build castles in the sky

To say that a person wants "to build castles in the sky" means that they have unrealistic or impractical plans or ideas. It suggests that the person is constructing something that is not based in reality and has no solid foundation. This phrase is often used to criticize someone for being overly optimistic or for having unrealistic expectations. This idiom originated in the 1500s and evolved from the original phrase "to build castles in Spain." During this time, much of Spain was under Moorish* control and the idea of building a castle there was considered to be an unattainable dream.

*During the Middle Ages, the term "Moor" was utilized by Christian Europeans to denote the Muslim inhabitants of the Maghreb, the Iberian Peninsula, Sicily, and Malta.

95. Blessing in disguise

The idiom "blessing in disguise" refers to something that seems bad or unfortunate at first, but ultimately turns out to have a positive outcome or result. The origin of this phrase can be traced back to the hymn, "Since all the downward tracts of time" by James Hervey, which was first published in 1746. In this hymn, Hervey meditated on the wisdom of accepting whatever God chose to bestow on us, even things that seemed negative or undesirable at first, because they might ultimately be "blessings in disguise," or good things that were initially difficult to recognize as such due to their appearance or circumstances. This expression has been in use since the mid-1700s and is a way of looking on the bright side of a challenging situation and finding the silver lining within.

96. Hunker down

The term "hunker down" has its origins in the American South in the 19th century, and is believed to be derived from the Scottish word "hunk," meaning to crouch or huddle. Initially used as a hunting term, describing the act of crouching low to the ground to avoid detection from prey, it gradually transitioned to a more general meaning of settling in for a long wait or preparing for a difficult situation. During World War II, soldiers were instructed to "hunker down" in trenches to avoid enemy fire, which further popularized the phrase. Today, it is commonly used to describe the act of preparing for a challenge or bracing oneself for a difficult situation, whether it be a natural disaster, a tough project, or a trying period in life.

97. In two shakes of a lamb's tail

The phrase "in two shakes of a lamb's tail" is a colloquial expression that originated in the early 19th century. The idiom is thought to be a variation of "in two shakes of a dead lion's tail" which was used to indicate something that would happen quickly or without delay. The phrase is used to indicate something that will happen quickly or immediately, similar to how fast a lamb's tail can be shaken twice. Interestingly, the term "shake" is an informal unit of time, which was first named and defined by the scientists working on the Manhattan Project*. These scientists designated a shake to be equal to ten nanoseconds, as they needed to be able to measure time in small increments in order to describe nuclear reactions. The earliest known publication of the expression "in two shakes of a lamb's tail" was in *Ingoldsby Legends* by Richard Barham in 1840. However, it is likely that the phrase is older than that, but its exact etymology is currently unknown.

*The Manhattan Project was a top-secret research and development program during World War II, which resulted in the creation of the world's first nuclear weapons. The project was headed by the United States and received support from the United Kingdom and Canada.

98. Over my dead body

If someone utters the phrase "over my dead body," it means that they strongly oppose or object to something. It is often used to express determination to prevent something from happening. The term may have originated in the 16th century, and it is said to have been used by knights when discussing the treasure that they had sworn to protect. In this context, the saying suggests that the enemy would have to walk over their dead body to reach the treasure. This is not the common usage of the expression, and it is not the way in which it is now used. Today, the idiom is often used in a more dramatic or exaggerated way to express strong opposition or determination, and it's not meant to be taken literally.

99. Couch potato

The term "couch potato" is used to describe a person who is lazy and inactive, often spending most of their time sitting on a couch watching television. It originated in the 1970s in America, coined by a comic artist who drew two idle and lazy characters which he named "Couch Potatoes." The phrase quickly caught on and is now commonly used to refer to those who lead a sedentary lifestyle. The term "couch potato" is a playful and humorous way of describing someone who is lazy and inactive, and is often used in a lighthearted or teasing manner.

100. Jump ship

If someone is ready to "jump ship" then they are about to abandon a situation, particularly a job or a project, without warning. The origin of this phrase comes from the practice of sailors deserting a ship, often by jumping off into the water and swimming to shore. This was a dangerous and potentially deadly action, as sailors could be left stranded in the middle of the ocean or face harsh punishment if caught. The expression became popular as a metaphor for leaving a situation in the early 20th century, and has been in common usage since then.

Did You Know?

The longest words in the English language are:

- Honorificabilitudinitatibus (twenty-seven letters) is a word that refers to the state of being able to achieve honor. It is not a commonly used word and is mostly found in lists of long words or in discussions about the history of the English language.
- Antidisestablishmentarianism (twenty-eight letters) refers to opposition to the disestablishment of the Church of England, especially in the 19th century. This word is not often used in everyday conversation, but it may come up in discussions about the history of the Church of England or the separation of church and state.
- Floccinaucinihilipilification (twenty-nine letters) is a word that refers to the act of estimating something as worthless. It is not a commonly used word and is mostly found in lists of long words.
- Supercalifragilisticexpialidocious (thirty-four letters) is a word that is used to describe something extraordinary or wonderful. It is famously used in the song "Supercalifragilisticexpialidocious" from the movie *Mary Poppins*. The word is not used often in everyday conversation, but it is recognized by many people due to the popular song.
- Pneumonoultramicroscopicsilicovolcanoconiosis (forty-five letters) is a technical term used to describe a lung disease caused by inhaling very fine silica particles. It is not a commonly used word and is often listed as one of the longest words in the English language.

101. Have the blues

To "have the blues" means you have a feeling of sadness or melancholy. It originated in the United States in the early 20th century, specifically in African American communities in the southern states. The phrase is thought to be derived from the musical genre known as the blues, which emerged at around the same time and is characterized by its emotive, soulful lyrics and themes of heartbreak, loneliness, and the struggles of daily life. It is possible that the expression was originally used to describe someone who was feeling down or depressed, possibly because they were listening to or performing blues music. Over time, the phrase became more popular and came to be used more broadly to describe any feeling of sadness or depression. Today, the idiom is commonly used in casual conversation to refer to a general feeling of melancholy, regardless of its connection to the blues genre.

102. Kill the goose that lays the golden eggs

This idiom originates from one of Aesop's fables. In the story, a farmer and his wife are in possession of a goose that lays golden eggs. Due to their greed, they decide to kill the goose, believing there would be more gold inside. Upon doing so, they discover that the goose is normal inside, and they have destroyed the one thing that was providing for them. Today, the phrase is used more broadly to mean to destroy or ruin something valuable or lucrative through greed or short-sightedness. It is often used to criticize the tendency to try to extract more significant, more immediate profits rather than accepting smaller, steady gains.

103. Clean bill of health

The idiom "clean bill of health" is used to describe a state of good physical or mental health. It is thought to have originated in the 16th century. The phrase likely came from the concept of a "bill of health," a document issued by a doctor or other medical professional attesting to the good health of an individual. In the past, it was common for people to travel long distances or spend extended periods of time away from home, and a "bill of health" was used to demonstrate that they were in good health and not carrying any diseases that could be transmitted to others. Today, the phrase "clean bill of health" is used more broadly to describe any state of good physical or mental health. It is often used in a positive or complimentary way, implying that the person is free of any major health issues or concerns. However, it can also be used more generally to describe any situation in which an individual or entity is deemed to be in good health or functioning properly.

104. Food for thought

The idiomatic phrase "food for thought" is used to describe something that is thought-provoking or that requires consideration or contemplation. It's believed to have originated in the early 17th century and is thought to be a reference to the idea of nourishing the mind as food nourishes the body. It is often used to suggest that the information or ideas presented are intellectually stimulating, offering new perspectives or insights. An alternative theory suggests that the phrase might have been derived from the practice of medieval scholars who would discuss serious matters over a meal. The discussions would be considered as "food" for the mind, hence the expression "food for thought." Regardless of its origin, the phrase is often used to introduce a topic or idea that is complex or difficult to understand. It is commonly used in educational or philosophical discussions, literature, and in everyday conversations to indicate that the speaker or writer is offering information or ideas that require further reflection and consideration.

105. Hold out an olive branch

The phrase "hold out an olive branch" is used to describe the act of offering peace, reconciliation, or forgiveness to someone. It has a rich history dating back to ancient Greece and Egypt, where the olive branch was regarded as a symbol of peace or victory. In Greece, olive branches were used by supplicants (a person who asks a god or someone who is in a position of power for something in a humble way) to show their status when visiting temples or approaching people of a higher rank. The olive branch also appears in Greek mythology, such as in the competition between Athena and Poseidon when they fought over the possession of Athens. Athena took possession after planting the first olive tree beside a well. Furthermore, olive wreaths have also been worn and awarded to Olympic victors. Today, it appears on the Great Seal of the United States as well as on the flag of Cyprus, symbolizing peace and victory.

106. In over his head

There are a few theories about the origin of the idiom "in over his head." One possible explanation is that it originated from the practice of diving or swimming. If a person is "in over his head," it could mean that they are in water that is too deep for them, and they may be in danger of drowning. In this context, being in over one's head could refer to being in a situation beyond one's depth or ability to handle it. Another theory is that the phrase may have originated from horse racing. In this context, "in over his head" could refer to a horse running too fast for its rider to control, leading the rider to be "in over his head." Finally, the phrase could simply be a figurative way of saying that someone is in a situation that is too difficult or complex for them to handle. In this case, the phrase is used to describe someone who is facing challenges or problems that are beyond their ability to cope with. Regardless of its exact origin, the idiom is now widely used to describe someone facing a situation beyond their ability to handle.

107. Can of worms

"Can of worms" is a vivid idiom used to describe a situation that, once opened, leads to unforeseen and complicated problems or challenges. We use this expression when referring to issues or topics that, when addressed, create a cascade of difficulties or controversies. Its origins can be traced back to fishing practices, where worms were stored in cans, and opening one could unleash a squirming mess. The first known use in writing was in the book *Beware of Pity* by Stefan Zweig in 1939. Over time, the phrase has evolved into a metaphor, symbolizing the complexity and unpredictability of delving into certain subjects or situations. Today, we use it to caution against casually approaching sensitive or intricate matters, understanding that opening a "can of worms" may lead to unintended consequences.

108. Lose one's touch

"To lose one's touch" is a phrase that has its origins in the artistic and creative fields, specifically in the realm of music and art. It alludes to the older sense of touch as a musician's skill on an instrument or an artist's skill in using a brush or chisel. The phrase likely originated from the idea that a person who was once highly skilled and proficient in a particular task or activity has now lost that ability due to various reasons such as age, lack of practice, or other factors. The phrase can be traced back to the 19th century, where it was used to describe musicians who had lost their virtuosity or artists who had lost their ability to produce striking works. In modern times it's used to express disappointment or to point out that someone has lost their former skill or ability.

109. Change of heart

"Change of heart" is a captivating idiom that refers to a profound shift in someone's feelings, beliefs, or opinions. We use this expression when describing a sudden or significant change in one's perspective or emotions. Its origins can be traced back to ancient times when the heart was believed to be the center of emotions and thoughts. The earliest known use in writing is in Shakespeare's *Twelfth Night* in 1602, where the character Viola experiences a change of heart towards her love interest. Over time, the expression has evolved into a metaphor for personal transformation and reconsideration of deeply-held convictions. Today, we use it to acknowledge personal growth, altered viewpoints, or newfound compassion.

110. Don't count your chickens before they hatch

"Don't count your chickens before they hatch" is a delightful expression that cautions against premature optimism or assuming a favorable outcome before it's certain. We use this idiom to advise against making plans or celebrating success prematurely, as unforeseen events can alter the expected outcome. Its origins can be traced back to Aesop's fables, specifically *The Milkmaid and Her Pail*, written around 600 BC. The exact first use in its current form is unclear, but variations appeared in literature throughout history. Over time, the phrase has evolved into a metaphorical reminder to stay grounded, temper expectations, and avoid overconfidence. Today, we use it playfully to remind ourselves and others that while optimism is valuable, it's equally important to be patient and realistic, awaiting the true fruition of our efforts.

Did You Know?

The magnificent "Big 5" animals represent the largest and most renowned creatures that roam the African continent. This esteemed group consists of:

Lions: Often hailed as the "kings of the jungle," lions possess an unmistakable majesty, commanding respect and admiration throughout Africa.

Elephants: Towering above all other land animals, elephants claim the title of the world's largest. Renowned for their intelligence and gentle demeanor, they embody a captivating grace.

Buffalos: Unyielding and formidable, African buffalos exude an air of unpredictability with their sheer size and intimidating presence. Their robust nature commands both fear and awe.

Leopards: The leopard, a master of stealth and strength, reigns as a mighty predator. Its adaptable hunting skills enable it to thrive in diverse environments, while its exquisite spotted coat adds to its allure.

Rhinoceros: An imposing sight to behold, the rhinoceros captivates with its immense stature. Its unmistakable horn, tragically coveted by poachers, symbolizes the battle for its survival. Africa is home to two rhinoceros species: the black and the white.

111. The genie is out of the bottle

The expression "the genie is out of the bottle" conveys that something has been released that cannot be easily controlled or undone. The phrase is a reference to the genie in the tale of Aladdin and the magic lamp. The story goes that when Aladdin rubs the magic lamp, a genie appears and grants him three wishes. But once the genie is released from the lamp, he can't be put back in, and the same applies to the idiom. It's often used in situations where people have made a mistake or when something has been released that can't be controlled, such as information that has been leaked to the public.

112. Ignorance is bliss

The expression "ignorance is bliss" means that not knowing about something can be more comfortable or pleasant than knowing about it. The saying is often attributed to Thomas Gray's poem *Ode on a Distant Prospect of Eton College*, which was published in 1742. In the poem, the line "Where ignorance is bliss, 'tis folly to be wise" appears, expressing the idea that it is sometimes better not to know certain things. However, the idea of ignorance being blissful dates back even further, to the work of the English philosopher Thomas Hobbes. In his work *Leviathan*, which was published in the 16th century, Hobbes wrote, "Ignorance of facts is the cause of fear." While it is generally considered better to have knowledge than ignorance, it is also true that no one knows everything, and it is natural for people to be unaware or ignorant of certain things.

113. Dig deep

The origin of "dig deep" as an idiom comes from the late 19th century when miners would literally dig deep into the earth in order to extract valuable resources, such as coal or gold. The phrase is often used as a metaphor to describe the process of making a sustained effort or putting in extra effort to achieve a goal or overcome a challenge. It's also used to describe the process of searching within oneself for inner strength or to investigate/research in great detail and with great effort.

114. Have bigger fish to fry

To "have bigger fish to fry" refers to a situation in which someone has more important or pressing matters to attend to and therefore cannot deal with something else. It probably originated in the 19th century and is derived from the idea of frying fish, which was a common method of cooking at the time. In this context, the phrase referred to the person doing the cooking, prioritizing the larger fish to fry as it would provide more of a meal. Nowadays, the phrase is used in a broad set of circumstances to convey that the speaker doesn't want to make the time for a side project or a distraction, as they "have bigger fish to fry" and need to focus.

115. It's all downhill from here

"It's all downhill from here" means that things will get easier or more successful from this point forward. It is often used to describe a situation where one has reached a bar or certain level of accomplishment, and things are expected to run more smoothly and with less headache from this point on. The metaphor suggests that one has reached the top of a hill and that things will now get easier as they go downhill. This phrase is often used to express a feeling of relief or satisfaction that one has overcome a difficult challenge and can now relax or enjoy the rewards of their hard work.

116. Keep a stiff upper lip

The phrase "keep a stiff upper lip" means to remain calm, composed, and unemotional, especially in difficult or trying situations. The phrase is often used to encourage someone to maintain their composure and not show weakness or vulnerability. The origins of the phrase are British, dating back to the 19th century. The phrase is thought to have originated from the British tradition of maintaining a stoic and unemotional facade, particularly during times of stress and hardship. It became popular and widespread during the Victorian Era, when British society valued self-control, stoicism and repressing emotions.

117. Firing on all cylinders

The expression "firing on all cylinders" originated from the internal combustion engine, specifically the four-stroke engine which was invented in 1876. In a four-stroke engine, there are four cylinders that work together to generate power and drive the vehicle. When all four cylinders are working efficiently and effectively, the engine is said to be "firing on all cylinders." The phrase was first used in print in the early 1900s and today is used to describe a situation where everything is working well and at full capacity. The phrase can also be used to describe a person or team who is performing at their best and achieving great results.

118. Get your act together

To "get your act together" means to organize and improve oneself or one's affairs. It is often used as a way to encourage someone to become more efficient or effective, or to resolve problems or issues that they are facing. The phrase suggests the idea of putting on a performance or show, and preparing all the necessary elements in order to put on a successful performance. The expression "get your act together" has its roots in the entertainment industry, where it was used to encourage actors who were feeling anxious or making errors to improve their performance. It has been used since the second half of the 1900s. This idiom is often used in a casual or informal setting, usually to encourage or motivate someone to take action to improve their situation. It can also be used as a way to show support or offer encouragement to someone who is facing challenges or difficulties.

119. Have the last laugh

Perhaps you've heard "have the last laugh" and "he who laughs last laughs best." These two sayings are basically the same and they mean to ultimately triumph or succeed, often after facing challenges or setbacks. It suggests that the person or group in question persevered or overcame adversity, and their perseverance has ultimately paid off. The expression was first used in a play called *The Christmas Prince* around 1608: "Laugh on laugh on my friend. Hee laugheth best that laugheth to the end."

120. Penny wise and pound foolish

The expression "penny-wise and pound foolish" means being careful or thrifty in small matters while being wasteful or extravagant in larger ones. It is often used to describe someone who is overly focused on saving small amounts of money while neglecting to consider the bigger picture or the long-term consequences of their actions. The phrase originated in the 17th century and is derived from the old English currency system, in which "penny" referred to small denominations of money, while "pounds" referred to larger denominations.

Did You Know?

The fastest animals in the world are incredibly unique and fascinating creatures. From land to water and even the sky, each of these animals have evolved in their own way to reach incredible speeds and survive in their environments.

On land, the cheetah reigns supreme as the fastest animal, capable of reaching speeds of up to 75 mph (120 km/hr). This slender and long-legged big cat has evolved with a flexible spine, non-retractable claws, and an enlarged heart and lungs, allowing it to hunt primarily during the day and catch smaller antelopes such as gazelles.

In the ocean, the sailfish holds the title of the fastest fish. Found in the Atlantic, Indian, and Pacific Oceans, these predatory fish are known for their long bill (rostrum) and sail-like dorsal fin. They are capable of reaching speeds of up to 68 mph (110 km/hr) and feed on smaller fish and squid.

Finally, in the sky, the peregrine falcon is the fastest bird in the world, diving at speeds of over 240 mph (386 km/hr). These birds of prey can be found on every continent except Antarctica and feed primarily on birds, such as pigeons and ducks, which they hunt in midair.

121. Find one's feet

The expression "to find one's feet" refers to becoming confident and secure in one's abilities or situation. Its origins are unclear, but it likely comes from the idea of a person becoming physically stable and finding direction. The phrase is related to the saying "to stand on one's own two feet" which means to be self-sufficient and independent. The earliest recorded use of the phrase was in 1817, in James Boswell's *The Life of Samuel Johnson* where he wrote: "He was now, however, enabled to find his feet, and to establish himself in the world."

122. Hit the sack

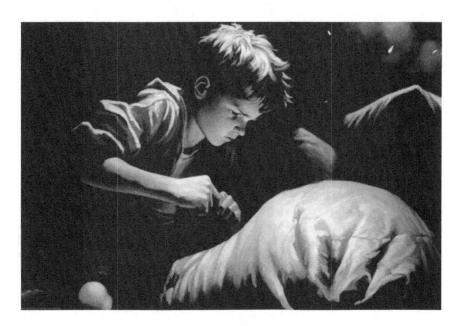

"Hit the sack" is an idiom that means to go to bed or to sleep. It originated in the 20th century and may have originally been used to describe the act of going to bed for the night or to take a nap. In modern usage, the phrase often describes the feeling of being tired or ready for bed. The phrase is thought to have been inspired by the idea of climbing into a bed or sleeping bag, which is sometimes referred to as a "sack."

123. Through thick and thin

The idiom "through thick and thin" means to support or remain loyal to someone or something in good times and bad. It is often used to describe a strong, enduring relationship or a commitment to a cause. The metaphor suggests that, just as one experiences both thick and thin slices of bread or bacon, one should be prepared to support and stand by someone through both good and bad times. The earliest written use of this phrase dates back to the late 16th century. It appears in a play called *The Two Gentlemen of Verona* by William Shakespeare, which was first performed in 1594.

124. Right as rain

The expression "right as rain" is used to describe someone or something that is in good condition or working properly. It originated in the United Kingdom in the 19th century and comes from the idea of rain being a natural and necessary part of the environment. When it's raining, the weather is generally considered to be normal and healthy. The phrase suggests that the person or thing in question is in a similar state of proper function. Today, it's used in a positive or complimentary way, implying that the person or thing is working as it should be and isn't experiencing any problems.

125. In the heat of the moment

"In the heat of the moment" is a vivid idiom used to describe impulsive or emotional actions taken during intense circumstances. We use it when referring to decisions made hastily, often under the influence of strong feelings or pressures. Its origins can be traced back to the late 19th century when "heat" symbolized the fervor or intensity of emotions. The earliest known use in writing was in Charles Reade's novel *A Terrible Temptation* in 1871. Over time, the expression has evolved into a metaphor for temporary lapses in judgment or behavior during heightened situations. Today, we use it to explain and understand actions that may not reflect our usual demeanor.

126. Sticks and stones

The famous line "sticks and stones may break my bones, but words will never hurt me" is a saying that has been used for centuries to remind people that words, even hurtful ones, cannot physically harm us. The phrase first appeared in *The Christian Recorder*, (1862) a publication of the African Methodist Episcopal Church, where it is presented as an "old adage" in this form: "Sticks and stones may break my bones, but words will never break me." This version of the phrase emphasizes the resilience and strength that one can gain from ignoring hurtful words. Soon after, the phrase also appeared in 1872, in the book *Tappy's Chicks* by Mrs. George Cupples. In this version, the phrase is presented as advice, stating: "Sticks and stones may break my bones, But names will never harm me."

127. Back against the wall

"Back against the wall" is an idiom that means to be in a challenging situation. It originated in the 16th century to describe the idea of being in a difficult situation with few resources available. The phrase is probably inspired by the idea of being physically cornered or trapped, with one's back literally against a wall and no way to escape. In modern usage, it's often used to explain situations where someone is facing a challenging situation and is feeling threatened with few options available.

128. Keep your fingers crossed

"Keep your fingers crossed" is a delightful idiom that conveys the hope for good luck or a favorable outcome. We use it when we want to express our optimistic anticipation for something positive to happen. Its origins can be traced back to ancient times when crossing one's fingers was believed to ward off evil spirits and bring good fortune. The earliest known use in writing was in the 1920s in a letter from author Thomas Hardy. Over time, the idiom has evolved into a playful gesture and a symbol of hopefulness. Today, we use it in various situations, from wishing someone luck before an important event to maintaining hope during uncertain times.

129. Que sera sera

The idiom "que sera, sera" is a phrase of Spanish origin, meaning "what will be, will be." It is commonly said to express acceptance of fate or the future, and a lack of control over the outcome of events. The phrase is often translated into English as "whatever will be, will be." The phrase originated in the 16th century, and it became popular in the 1950s with the release of a song titled "Que Sera, Sera (Whatever Will Be, Will Be)" which was written by Jay Livingston and Ray Evans and sung by Doris Day. The song was featured in the 1956 Alfred Hitchcock film *The Man Who Knew Too Much*. The song became a hit and it helped to popularize the phrase. In modern times, it is possible to say "que sera, sera" as a way to encourage someone to let go of their worries or concerns and to trust that things will work out in the end.

130. Dead man walking

The phrase "dead man walking" refers to a person who is in a hopeless or helpless situation, usually one in which imminent death or severe punishment are right around the corner. The phrase is thought to have originated in the American prison system in the 1900s, specifically to mean a man who is condemned to death or is slated for execution. It was popularized in the 1990s through the book and movie *The Green Mile* and the nonfiction book *Dead Man Walking* by Sister Helen Prejean, a Catholic nun and anti-death penalty activist.

Did You Know?

The Colosseum was built in 80 AD and was one of the largest amphitheaters in the ancient world. The Colosseum was built on the site of an artificial lake near the center of Rome and was capable of seating fifty thousand spectators. The building was a major engineering feat and its construction involved the use of concrete and stone as well as a complex system of underground passages and rooms. The Colosseum was used for a variety of purposes, including gladiatorial games, animal hunts, and public spectacles.

Gladiators were professional fighters, often slaves or prisoners of war. They were trained to fight in the arena and they were often forced into this dangerous and brutal profession. Some gladiators were free men who had voluntarily signed up for the life of a gladiator in exchange for fame and fortune. They were highly valued for their skills and bravery and some became popular celebrities in ancient Rome.

The last recorded gladiatorial games in the Colosseum were held in the 5th century AD. Its popularity declined in the later years of the Roman Empire and the last recorded games in the Colosseum were held in the 5th century AD. The building was later used for various purposes, such as housing, workshops, and even a religious shrine. The Colosseum remains one of the most iconic symbols of Ancient Rome and its legacy as a center of power and spectacle.

131. Keep your head above water

The expression "keep your head above water" means to survive or maintain one's position or status despite challenging circumstances. It suggests the need to struggle or work hard in order to stay afloat or avoid being overwhelmed by the demands of a situation. There are a few possible origins for this phrase, including the idea of literally keeping one's head above water to avoid drowning and the idea of being in a difficult financial or economic situation. Today, the phrase is used more broadly to express the need to struggle or work hard in order to stay afloat or avoid being overwhelmed by the demands of a situation.

132. Beyond the pale

The phrase "beyond the pale" means something is outside the bounds of acceptability or appropriateness. The origin of this phrase comes from the 14th century from the medieval practice of marking the boundaries of a town or city with a fence or wall, known as a "pale." Anything outside of this boundary was considered to be in a lawless or uncivilized area, and anything or anyone "beyond the pale" was considered to be outside of the protection or jurisdiction of the authorities.

There's another idiom with the word "pale" which is "pale in comparison." This expression means to be inferior or less significant in comparison to something else. The origin of this phrase comes from the idea of something being less vivid or colorful in comparison.

133. Curiosity killed the cat

"Curiosity killed the cat" is used to express the idea that being too curious or inquisitive can lead to trouble or danger. It is a cautionary warning against being overly nosy or meddlesome. The phrase suggests that a cat's curiosity could lead to its demise, as cats are known for their curiosity. The saying originated in a play written by Ben Johnson in 1598, where the original wording was "care killed the cat," but the modern usage with "curiosity" was first recorded in 1873.

134. The tail wags the dog

The phrase "the tail wags the dog" means that a small or insignificant part of something is controlling or dominating the whole. It's often in situations where the means or the method of achieving a goal becomes more important than the goal itself. It originated in the US in the late 19th century and there are a few different theories about the starting points of this phrase. One theory is that it comes from the idea of a dog wagging its tail, which is a small part of the dog but can still have a significant effect on the dog's overall behavior. Another theory is that the phrase is related to the idea of a small group or minority having a disproportionate amount of influence or control over a larger group or majority. Today, the idiom is often used in a negative or critical way, implying that a situation is not functioning properly.

135. Ivory tower

The term "ivory tower" has a rich history of meaning and usage. In the Bible, it is used in the Song of Solomon to depict a woman's purity and her secluded, protected state. However, the modern understanding of the phrase as a term for someone who is detached from reality and living in a world of ideals or unrealistic dreams is believed to have originated in France in the 1830s with the term "tour d'ivoire" which means an impractical dreamer. The phrase was later adopted in the English language in the late 1800s, with the meaning possibly reinforced by the Hawksmoor Towers at Oxford University's All Souls' College, which were close to an ivory color at the time the term was introduced. Another theory suggests that the phrase originated from the German word "Eigenturm" which means "self-tower" and was used to describe the secluded and isolated lifestyle of certain scholars in the Middle Ages.

136. Hem and haw

To "hem and haw" means you are reluctant to give a direct answer. This can be done by providing long-winded responses without actually saying anything or by using what is known as filler sounds such as 'um,' 'er,' or 'uh.' The expression was first used in the poem *My Lady's Lamentation* by Jonathan Swift in 1728, with the line: "He haws and he hums. At last out it comes." The expression is dependent on the definitions of the two words. To 'hem' is a term from the late 1400s, meaning making a noise in the throat to get someone's attention. This can be done in a polite, gentle way, or it can be done rudely. 'Hawing' dates to the 1600s and is a sound of hesitation.

137. Cry for the moon

The idiom "cry for the moon" means to want something that is impossible or unattainable. It is often a way to describe a person who is being unrealistic or unreasonable in their demands or expectations. The metaphor suggests that it is as futile to cry for the moon as it is to try to obtain something that is impossible or beyond one's grasp. The earliest written use of this phrase dates back to the early 20th century. It appears in a book called *A Dictionary of Modern English Usage* by H.W. Fowler, which was published in 1926. The book defines the phrase as "to demand the impossible; to wish for what cannot be obtained."

138. Get back in the saddle

The idiom "get back in the saddle" embodies the act of resuming an activity after a period of inactivity or overcoming a setback to forge ahead. Its roots can be traced to the 1800s, originating from the realm of horseback riding. In this context, it denoted the act of a rider remounting a horse after being thrown off, displaying resilience and determination. The mental image conjured is that of a jockey or cowboy who, despite being dislodged from their steed, promptly returns to the saddle, resuming their ride. This phrase carries a profound message, advising that when one encounters a fall or setback, the immediate response should be to confront the challenges head-on. By doing so, one gains mastery over both the temperament of the horse and the fears that may have arisen. Its usage extends beyond equestrian pursuits, serving as a metaphor for resilience and tenacity in the face of adversity.

139. All in the same boat

The phrase "all in the same boat" means that everyone is facing the same situation or problem, and their fates are interconnected. We use it to emphasize shared circumstances or challenges, highlighting that no one is exempt from the consequences. This saying likely originated from the maritime world, where passengers or crew members on a boat or ship share a common fate, for better or worse. Its first use in writing is challenging to pinpoint, but variations of the expression can be found in historical texts and literature, dating back centuries. Over time, the idiom has evolved to encompass various contexts beyond the maritime setting, emphasizing solidarity, collective responsibility, or shared experiences in different situations. Today, we use it to remind ourselves and others that we are all interconnected and that the outcomes of our actions impact not only ourselves but also those around us.

140. Water under the bridge

The expression "water under the bridge" means that a past event or issue has been resolved, forgiven, or forgotten, and it no longer has any effect on the present. We use it when we want to indicate that there's no use dwelling on something that has already happened and cannot be changed. The origins of this idiom can be traced back to the idea of water flowing continuously under a bridge, symbolizing the passage of time and the irreversibility of past events. While its exact first use in writing remains uncertain, similar phrases appeared in literature and oral traditions throughout history. Over time, its meaning has evolved to emphasize moving on from the past, learning from experiences, and focusing on the present and the future. Today, we use it to encourage resilience and a positive outlook, acknowledging that some things are best left behind.

Did You Know?

Babylon was one of the world's first great cities located in Mesopotamia (modern-day Iraq). Babylon was founded around 2300 BC and quickly grew into one of the most influential cities of the ancient world. It was strategically located at the crossroads of important trade routes and became a hub for commerce and culture.

Over time, Babylon grew in power and became the capital of the Babylonian Empire, which controlled much of Mesopotamia and beyond. The empire was ruled by powerful kings, including Nebuchadnezzar II, who is best known for his role in the Babylonian Captivity of the Jews.

The Hanging Gardens of Babylon were one of the Seven Wonders of the Ancient World and they were a marvel of engineering and beauty. The gardens were built by Nebuchadnezzar II for his queen, who missed the lush green landscapes of her homeland, and they were said to have been a series of terraces with exotic plants and flowing water.

The Babylonians were a highly educated and advanced civilization and they made important contributions to fields such as astronomy, mathematics, and literature. They created a sophisticated system of writing, known as cuneiform, which was used for record-keeping, literature, and mathematics. They also made important contributions to the field of astronomy, including the development of a highly accurate lunar calendar.

The Babylonians were known for their strict system of law and order, which was codified in the famous *Code of Hammurabi*. This law code, which was inscribed on a stele, outlined the rights and responsibilities of citizens and dealt with topics such as property, trade, and criminal punishment. The *Code of Hammurabi* was one of the first written legal codes and remains an important artifact for our understanding of ancient Babylonian society.

141. Sights set on

The expression "to have one's sights set on" originated from the practice of using a gun's sights to aim at a target. When a person aims a gun, they align the front and rear sights on the gun with the target, ensuring that the bullet will hit the desired location when fired. In this way, the idiom "to have one's sights set on" has come to mean to be focused on or determined to achieve a particular goal, as if the goal is the target that the person is aiming for.

142. A snowball effect

"A snowball effect" refers to a situation in which a small or insignificant actions lead to a series of larger or more significant events or consequences. It originated in the 19th century and is derived from the idea of a snowball rolling downhill and gaining size and speed as it goes. Today, the phrase is often used to convey a sense of momentum or escalation.

143. Penny for your thoughts

"Penny for your thoughts" is a delightful idiom used to playfully inquire about someone's thoughts or feelings. We use this expression when we want to know what someone is thinking, especially during moments of contemplation or reflection. Its origins can be traced back to medieval England, where the phrase "a penny for your thought" was used as a lighthearted way of asking for someone's opinion or inner musings. The earliest known use in writing was in John Heywood's *A Dialogue Conteinyng the Number in Effect of All the Prouerbes in the Englishe Tongue* in 1546. Over time, the idiom has evolved into a charming and friendly way of engaging in conversation, often used as an icebreaker or a casual invitation to share thoughts.

144. Slip of the tongue

A "slip of the tongue" refers to an unintentional mistake or error made in speech. It is often used to describe an unintentional verbal slip-up, such as a misspoken word or phrase. The phrase might be said in a humorous or lighthearted manner, but it can also be utilized in a more serious context to describe a mistake that has serious consequences. The phrase "slip of the tongue" is thought to be derived from the Latin phrase "lapsus linguae," which translates to "a slip of the tongue." This phrase was used by scholars and theologians of the time to describe an unintentional error made in speech.

145. The world is one's oyster

The saying "the world is one's oyster" means that everything is possible or that one has the opportunity to achieve anything they desire. The phrase originated from a line in Shakespeare's play *The Merry Wives of Windsor*, where a character named Pistol says "Why, then the world's mine oyster, Which I with sword will open." In this context, Pistol means that he is going to take whatever he wants, and the world is his to conquer. Later on, the phrase was reinterpreted to mean that the world is full of opportunities, and one can achieve anything they want with determination and hard work.

146. Knuckle down

To "knuckle down" means to focus intently on a task or goal and to apply oneself to it with determination and diligence. It suggests that the person or group in question is willing to put in the necessary effort and hard work to achieve their objectives and that they can handle challenges and setbacks. The phrase probably originated in the early 19th century and is believed to be related to a physical gesture of bending the knuckles down to the surface to signify readiness to work hard. It could also be related to the phrase "knuckle under" which means to submit or give in to pressure or authority. It's also spoken aloud to encourage someone to take a task more seriously and apply more effort.

147. Bad apple

The term "bad apple" or "rotten apple" refers to a person who is a
bad influence or a source of trouble within a group. It is thought to
have originated from the proverb "one bad apple (or rotten apple)
spoils the whole barrel." The earliest known version of this proverb
can be found in *The Cook's Tale* in Geoffrey Chaucer's *Canterbury Tales*
where he wrote: "About an old proverb, the words that say: 'A rotten
apple's better thrown away Before it spoils the barrel.'" This passage
shows that the expression was well known before Chaucer's time.
Proverbs are short, common sayings or phrases that particularly give
advice or share a universal truth, or impart wisdom. This phrase is
often used as a warning of the potential negative effects of having a
bad individual among a group.

148. Pull the wool over someone's eyes

"Pull the wool over someone's eyes" is a fascinating idiom used to describe deceiving or tricking someone, making them believe something that is not true. We use this expression when referring to the act of concealing the truth to manipulate or mislead another person. Its origins can be traced back to the 16th century when the phrase"wool over the eyes" alluded to blinding or obscuring someone's vision. The earliest known use in writing was in Samuel Butler's poem *Hudibras*, in 1663. Over time, the phrase has evolved into a figurative expression for cunning or clever deceit. Today, we use it in various contexts, from playful banter to serious warnings, to caution others against being duped or to share stories of clever manipulation.

149. Pour out one's heart

To "pour out one's heart" means to express one's innermost feelings, emotions, or thoughts openly and candidly. It is often used to describe someone who is expressing their feelings in a sincere and heartfelt way. The origin of this idiom is related to the idea of pouring out something that is contained within oneself, much like one might pour out a liquid from a container. The metaphor suggests that one is sharing their deepest, most personal thoughts and feelings in a candid manner. The earliest written use of this phrase dates back to the late 16th century and appears in a play called *Hamlet* by William Shakespeare, which was first performed in 1601. In the play, the character Hamlet speaks the line: "I have of late—but wherefore I know not—lost all my mirth, forgone all custom of exercises; and indeed it goes so heavily with my disposition that this goodly frame, the earth, seems to me a sterile promontory, this most excellent canopy, the air, look you, this brave o'erhanging firmament, this majestical roof fretted with golden fire, why, it appears no other thing to me than a foul and pestilent congregation of vapors."

150. The whole kit and caboodle

When you have "the whole kit and caboodle," it means that you have everything you need. This phrase originates from 18th century England where the word "kit" is derived from "kith," meaning estate; therefore, the "entire kith" refers to the estate and all its contents. Soldiers would also carry their belongings in a kitbag, also known as a "caboodle." Today, the phrase is used more broadly to mean everything or an entire set of things and is often used to refer to a large or diverse collection of items or elements. It suggests that everything is included or accounted for.

Did You Know?

Ancient Egypt thrived for over three thousand years, spanning from 3150 BC to 30 BC. The Ancient Egyptians demonstrated great expertise in medicine and surgery, utilizing diverse remedies like honey, aloe vera, and castor oil. Additionally, they practiced mummification to ensure the preservation of bodies for the afterlife, a meticulous process involving the removal of internal organs, treatment with preservatives, and enveloping in linen bandages. Their profound achievements also encompassed a sophisticated system of writing, mathematics, astronomy, and engineering, which would significantly influence subsequent civilizations, including Greece and Rome.

Amid the annals of the history of the Ancient Egyptians, the Rosetta Stone emerges as a captivating artifact. Discovered by French soldiers in 1799, this black basalt slab features inscriptions in three scripts: Greek, Demotic (an Egyptian script), and Hieroglyphic. Its inscriptions date back to a decree issued at Memphis in 196 BC. By virtue of the Greek script's decipherability, scholars found in the Rosetta Stone the key to unlocking the enigmatic Hieroglyphics, which had remained unreadable for over a millennium.

Venturing into the realm of decipherment, British scholar Thomas Young took the initial steps, successfully identifying a few names and words from the Hieroglyphics on the Rosetta Stone. However, it was the French scholar Jean-Francois Champollion who achieved a momentous breakthrough. Immersing himself in the inscriptions on the Rosetta Stone and other ancient Egyptian texts, Champollion discerned that Hieroglyphics comprised a blend of ideograms, representing objects or concepts, and phonograms, representing sounds.

With this profound revelation, Champollion skillfully unveiled the names of Pharaohs and gods in Hieroglyphics, eventually producing a comprehensive grammar and dictionary of the ancient Egyptian language. The Rosetta Stone, therefore, became a pivotal artifact, unraveling the long-guarded secrets of ancient Egypt and providing historians and archaeologists with invaluable insights into the language and culture of this enigmatic civilization.

151. One fell swoop

The phrase "one fell swoop" means to accomplish something in one swift and decisive action. The phrase was first seen in Shakespeare's play *Macbeth*, where the titular character Macbeth, who is a Scottish nobleman and warrior, is urged by three witches to murder King Duncan and take the throne for himself. Macbeth is initially hesitant but is eventually convinced by his wife to go through with the plan. He devises a scheme to kill King Duncan and his family in "one fell swoop," and he carries out the plan successfully. In Act 2, Scene 1, he says: "I have no spur to prick the sides of my intent, but only vaulting ambition, which overleaps itself and falls on the other. And this thought, too, is now a horse before the horse I follow, with bloody hoofs. That's all. The crown, and all will I to win in one fell swoop."

152. Eat your words

The idiomatic phrase "eat your words" is used to describe the act of retracting or taking back something that was said previously, especially when it was said confidently or boastfully. The phrase was first published in John Ray's *English Proverbs* in 1670. The way that this saying is used today has a negative connotation, referring to someone who is forced to retract or take back a statement they made. In Ezekiel 3:1-3, it means to feast on the word of the Lord, to take it in, as God told Ezekiel to eat the scroll he was given, and then go and speak to the people of Israel.

153. Knee-slapper

The term "knee-slapper" is a colloquialism that refers to a joke or story that is particularly funny and likely to make the listener slap their knee in response. The origins of the phrase are not clear, but it likely dates back to the early 20th century and may have been popularized in vaudeville (a theatrical genre of variety entertainment born in France at the end of the 19th century) and other forms of live entertainment where audiences would physically respond to jokes and comedic performances.

154. The apple doesn't fall far from the tree

The expression "the apple doesn't fall far from the tree" means that children often resemble or behave like their parents. It is used to suggest that a person's characteristics or traits are inherited or passed down from their parents. The earliest known appearance in print is from 1605 in a book called *Hieronymus Megiser*, in which multiple proverbs are listed. On page 65, the proverb is written in German as "Der Apffel fellt nicht weit vom Baum," which translates to "the apple does not fall far from the tree" in English. The phrase can be used as an insult or a compliment, depending on the characteristic that the offspring is exhibiting.

155. Back the wrong horse

The phrase "back the wrong horse" comes from the sport of horse racing, where it refers to placing a bet on a horse that ultimately loses the race. The idioms "back the wrong horse" and "bet on the wrong horse" are as old as horse racing itself, but they became particularly popular in the latter part of the 19th century. At that time, the idioms were often used to describe political races, as people would metaphorically "back" or "bet" on a certain candidate they thought would win, only to see them lose the election. The first recorded horse race is believed to have taken place in ancient Greece in 648 BC, during the ancient Olympic Games. These early horse races were chariot races, where teams of horses pulled chariots driven by charioteers. Horse racing as we know it today, where thoroughbred horses run on a track, began to take shape in England during the Middle Ages. The first recorded horse race that closely resembled modern horse racing took place in the 12th century at Smithfield, London. The sport was initially called "course de chevaux" (horse course) and was a popular pastime for the nobility and the royal family.

156. Shoot from the hip

The expression "shoot from the hip" means to act or speak impulsively or without careful consideration. It is commonly used to describe someone who is quick to act or speak, without taking the time to think things through or consider the consequences of their actions. The origin of this idiom is related to the practice of shooting a gun from the hip, rather than taking the time to aim and shoot more accurately. The earliest written use of this phrase dates back to the early 20th century. It appears in a book called *The American Language* by H.L. Mencken, which was published in 1919. The book includes the line, "To shoot from the hip is to act or speak impulsively, without taking the time to think things through."

157. Left to your own devices

This phrase originated in the 19th century and is derived from the verb "devise." While devise now means "to plan," its original meaning was "to desire." Today, the phrase is used more broadly to mean to be left to one's own resources or to be left to one's own methods and is often used to suggest that the person in question is free to act or do as they please, without interference or supervision from others. It can also describe a situation where a person is left to their own methods to achieve a goal or solve a problem and is free to use their own strategies without interference or supervision from others.

158. Birds of a feather flock together

"Birds of a feather flock together" is an idiom that can be traced back to ancient Greek literature and was derived from the observation that birds of the same species tend to congregate together. It means that people who are similar or have shared interests or characteristics tend to associate with one another. In modern usage, the phrase often describes situations where people who have similar backgrounds, interests, or beliefs tend to form close relationships. The phrase expresses the fact that people tend to seek out and associate with others who are similar to themselves, and that they may be more comfortable or feel more at home in the company of people who share their interests.

159. Finger in every pie

The expression "finger in every pie" refers to someone who is involved in many different activities or projects, often in a way that is seen as excessive or unnecessary. The origin of the phrase comes from the practice of putting a finger in a pie to test its quality or to taste it. The phrase has been in use since the 16th century and it was first recorded in 1546 in the book *A dialogue Conteinyng the Number in Effect of all the Prouerbes in the Englishe Tongue* by John Heywood; however, it's also found in Shakespeare's play *All's Well That Ends Well*.

160. In the ballpark

The phrase "in the ballpark" could have originated in one of two ways. One hypothesis suggests that it arose from baseball commentary, in which a commentator would approximate the size of the audience by observing the crowds within the stadium. Another theory suggests that it originated from the jargon of atomic weapons scientists, who first used the term in 1954 to indicate that a prediction or estimate was within an acceptable range of approximation, similar to the area within which a missile was expected to return to Earth. In modern usage, "in the ballpark" means a rough estimate or close enough to a number that it is acceptable.

Did You Know?

The Seven Wonders of the Ancient World were structures considered to be the most impressive and remarkable buildings of the ancient world. These seven wonders include:

1. The Great Pyramid of Giza (Egypt)
2. The Hanging Gardens of Babylon (Iraq)
3. The Statue of Zeus at Olympia (Greece)
4. The Temple of Artemis at Ephesus (Turkey)
5. The Mausoleum at Halicarnassus (Turkey)
6. The Colossus of Rhodes (Greece)
7. The Lighthouse of Alexandria (Egypt)

These wonders were chosen based on their size, beauty, and technological advancement, and only the Great Pyramid of Giza remains standing to this day as one of the oldest and most impressive structures in the world.

There are both ancient and modern Seven Wonders of the World. The ancient Seven Wonders of the World were compiled by ancient Greek historians, while the modern Seven Wonders of the World, also known as the "New Seven Wonders of the World," were selected through a global poll in the early 2000s. The modern Seven Wonders include:

1. The Great Wall (China)
2. Petra (Jordan)
3. Christ the Redeemer (Brazil)
4. Machu Picchu (Peru)
5. Chichen Itza (Mexico)
6. The Roman Colosseum (Italy)
7. The Taj Mahal (India)

161. Pull the rug out from under

The expression "to pull the rug out from under" means to suddenly withdraw support or to change the conditions of something, causing it to fail or collapse. The origin of the phrase is likely derived from the physical act of pulling a rug out from under someone's feet, causing them to stumble or fall. The metaphor implies that someone is causing a situation or a person to fail or lose stability. The earliest known example is a 1907 article in the *Salt Lake Tribune*, where a situation was detailed in which a political party withdrew their support for a candidate, causing their campaign to fail.

162. The ball is in your court

"The ball is in your court" is a clever idiom used to convey that it is someone else's turn to take action or make a decision in a particular situation. We use this expression when referring to a moment in a conversation or negotiation where the responsibility lies with the other person to respond or make a move. Its origins can be traced back to sports, particularly tennis, where players take turns hitting the ball back and forth. The earliest known use in writing was in the early 1900s when it was used in sports commentary. Over time, the phrase has evolved beyond the sports context and is now widely used in everyday conversations, business dealings, and personal interactions. Today, we use it to prompt others to make a decision or to emphasize their role in resolving a matter.

163. Drown one's sorrows

To "drown one's sorrows" is a colloquial way of describing the act of using alcohol or other substances as a means of coping with emotional pain or stress. The phrase originated in the late 19th century and the original expression seems to be "drown your sorrows in the flowing bowl." The origin of this phrase is believed to come from the idea of drowning or submerging something, in this case, one's sorrows or emotional pain, in an attempt to make them disappear or at least to dull the feelings associated with them. The use of alcohol as a means of coping with emotional pain is an age-old problem. It's important to note that using alcohol or other substances as a way to cope with emotional pain is not a healthy habit and it could lead to addiction and other problems. This phrase should be used with caution and it's important to seek professional help if you are struggling with addiction or emotional distress.

164. The proof is in the pudding

The idiom "the proof is in the pudding" is a well-established expression that connotes the principle that the value, quality, or truth of something must be assessed based on direct experience with it or on its results. This phrase is an alteration of an older adage, "the proof of the pudding is in the eating," which suggests that things must be evaluated by trying them oneself or observing them in action, rather than on other factors such as hearsay. Another variation of the term is "the proof of the pudding," which refers to the results themselves, direct experience with something, or the testing of something to judge its value or truth. In these phrases, the word "proof" was originally used in the sense of a test of something, such as a test of quality, worth, truth, and so on. However, it is now commonly interpreted as meaning the same thing as evidence.

165. Scot free

The term "scot-free" refers to someone who has escaped punishment or consequences for their actions. There are two theories for this idiom. The first is that the phrase originated in the 16th century from the Scottish legal system. In Scotland, there was a practice of giving a "scot" or a fine to those who had committed a crime. If someone managed to escape this fine, they were said to have gotten away "scot-free." A second theory of origin posits that the expression is derived from the Scandinavian term "Skat," which signifies "tax" or "payment." This word evolved into "scot" as a designation for redistributive taxation implemented for the alleviation of poverty during the 10th century. Those who were exempt from paying the tax were referred to as being "scot-free."

166. House of cards

The idiom "house of cards" is a metaphor for something that is built on a fragile or unstable foundation and is likely to collapse or fall apart easily. The phrase is thought to have originated in the 16th century, when card games that involved building houses or structures out of cards became popular. The game would be played by building a structure out of cards, and the player who built the tallest or most stable structure would be the winner. However, if a card was placed incorrectly or the structure was not balanced properly, the whole house would come tumbling down, hence the phrase "house of cards" referring to a fragile situation.

167.Break the bank

To "break the bank" refers to the act of using up all of one's resources or exceeding one's budget. It is believed to have originated from the game of craps, in which a player can win all of the money in the "bank" at the craps table by rolling a certain combination of dice. Some sources suggest that the phrase may have originated as early as 1600, when gamblers won more money than the house (bank) could afford to pay, or in 1873, when a roulette player won $350,000 (an enormous sum for the day) at Monte Carlo.

168. The pot calling the kettle black

"The pot calling the kettle black" is a humorous idiom used to highlight the irony of someone criticizing another person for a fault they possess themselves. We use this expression when referring to a situation where someone accuses another of something that they are equally guilty of, often to humorous effect. Its origins can be traced back to the 17th century when the phrase "the pot calls the pan burnt-arse" was used in a comedic play by Thomas Middleton. Over time, the idiom evolved into its current form, becoming a popular saying to point out hypocrisy or double standards. Today, we use it in a lighthearted manner to tease or remind someone of their own flaws while they criticize others.

169. It is always darkest before the dawn

The idiom "it is always darkest before the dawn" means that things are likely to get worse before they get better. It is often used to encourage someone to persevere through difficult times, as a reminder that the situation will eventually improve. The idea behind this phrase is from the darkest time of the night being just before the sun begins to rise. The metaphor suggests that just when things seem the bleakest, there is hope for improvement on the horizon. The earliest written use of this phrase dates back to the 16th century. It appears in a play called *The Spanish Tragedy* by Thomas Kyd, which was first published in 1592. In the play, the character Hieronimo speaks the line: "For woes are wont to work their own redress, As night does bring the day: It is most true, that musing meditation most doth hurt, and careful counsel turns to passion; but best it is, if after labor, rest come easily; it is a common thing, that very ills have their own kind of good; and very pains, a present joy; for still it is most true, that 'tis the darkest hour That the dawn doth show itself."

170. Go under the knife

The expression "go under the knife" means to undergo surgery. It originated in the United States in the early 20th century. It comes from the idea of surgery being a medical procedure in which a patient is placed under general anesthesia while a surgeon performs an operation using a knife or scalpel. The phrase suggests that the person in question is preparing to undergo surgery and will be "under the knife" of the surgeon. Today, the idiom is used to describe undergoing surgery or any other medical procedure that involves the use of a knife or other sharp instruments. It is often used in a casual or lighthearted manner, implying that the person is preparing to undergo a relatively minor or routine procedure but can also be used more seriously to describe a more complex or serious surgery.

Did You Know?

The wheel is one of the most important inventions of all time, transforming the way people transport goods, travel, and build structures. The wheel revolutionized transportation, allowing goods to be moved much more efficiently, and making it easier for people to travel long distances. The wheel has also had a significant impact on commerce, agriculture, and trade, allowing people to expand their reach and access new resources.

Electricity is a powerful force that has transformed nearly every aspect of modern life. From powering homes and businesses to providing energy for transportation and manufacturing, electricity has had a profound impact on the way people live, work, and interact with the world around them. Without electricity, many of the modern technologies we take for granted would not be possible, making it one of the most important and useful inventions of all time.

The Internet has revolutionized the way people communicate, access information, and do business. By connecting people from all over the world, the Internet has opened up new opportunities for education, commerce, and social interaction. The Internet has also created new industries and job opportunities and has been instrumental in driving technological innovations and scientific advancements. The Internet is one of the most important inventions of all time and its impact will continue to be felt for generations to come.

171. How do you like them apples

If someone asks you "how do you like them apples?" they are probably mocking you or making fun of a situation that has just occurred. This idiom is often used when someone wants to make a sarcastic or humorous comment about something that has happened or been revealed. There are various theories about the origin of this phrase, but one possible explanation is that it dates back to World War I. During this time, some grenades and mortars used in the war were nicknamed "apples," with one two-inch mortar nicknamed the "toffee apple" due to its appearance. Another theory suggests that the expression was first used in 1895 when it appeared in an article published in *The Eagle* newspaper. However, the phrase gained widespread popularity in modern culture after it was used in the film *Good Will Hunting* in 1997.

172. Get up the wrong side of the bed

The idiom "to get up on the wrong side of the bed" is used to describe someone who is in a bad mood. The phrase implies that a person's negative behavior is due to waking up on the wrong side of the bed. It usually is said in a light-hearted tone about someone who is grumpy, irritable, or easily annoyed. The origins of the expression come from the Roman Empire. The Romans had a superstition that the left side of the bed was the wrong side, and getting up on the left side of the bed would bring them bad luck for the day. This superstition was passed down through the centuries and eventually made its way into the modern phrase.

173. Know where the bodies are buried

The morbid phrase "to know where the bodies are buried" is a colloquial expression that means to have knowledge of hidden or secret information, especially information that could be damaging or incriminating if revealed. The phrase was first recorded in the column "*Something to Think About*," written by Bruno Lessing in *The Monroe News-Star* (Monroe, Louisiana) on April 6th, 1928. The quote from the article reads as follows: "It would not be fair to quote more from this book. But something ought to be done to suppress this chap. He knows too much about us. He knows where the body is buried."

174. At each other's throats

"At each other's throats" is an idiom that refers to a situation where two people or groups are in a state of hostility with one another. It originated in the 16th century and was used to describe physical confrontations or fights between two people, whether that was physical or verbal. Today, the phrase is often utilized as a way to describe the intensity or severity of a disagreement or conflict, and to suggest that the situation is becoming increasingly hostile or volatile.

175. You can't make an omelet without breaking some eggs

"You can't make an omelet without breaking some eggs" means that sometimes, in order to achieve a desired outcome, it's necessary to accept or endure some level of inconvenience. It originated in the 19th century and was used to describe the idea that achieving a goal or making progress often requires sacrifice. The phrase is often used to encourage people to be persistent or resilient in the face of challenges or setbacks, and to recognize that, sometimes, achieving an outcome requires a willingness to put in the effort or to accept the consequences of one's actions.

176. Even-stevens

The term "even-steven" or "even-stevens" is used to describe a situation where everything is fair and equal. It originated in the United States in the 19th century and is also used in British and Australian English. The phrase does not have any definitive origin, but it is believed to have come from a line in Jonathan Swift's *Journal to Stella*. Another theory suggests that "steven" or "stephen" was a British slang term for money, hence when two people are even-steven, their financial contributions are equal. The phrase should be written as "even-steven" or "even-stevens" and "steven" or "stevens" is not capitalized.

177. Don't run before you can walk

The expression "don't run before you can walk" is used to caution someone not to move on to more advanced or complex tasks or goals before they have achieved a basic level of proficiency in a particular area. The phrase is often used as a way to remind someone to take things step by step, and not to try to do too much too soon. The phrase is of relatively recent origin, having come about in the United States in the 20th century. The expression is similar to the one of "not putting the cart before the horse" which is also used to advise people not to proceed in an activity or task before the necessary foundation or prerequisite is in place.

178. Let sleeping dogs lie

"Let sleeping dogs lie" is an idiom that means to leave something alone, particularly if it is causing no harm or if addressing it might cause more problems than it solves. The origin of the phrase is thought to stem from Geoffrey Chaucer's poem *Troilus and Criseyde*, published in 1374, where it is written as "It is nought good a sleeping hound to wake." The saying was also used in French even earlier in the 14th century, in *Proverbia Vulgalia et Latina*, with the phrase "Ne reveillez pas le chien qui dort," which translates to "Do not wake the dog that sleeps."

179. The sky's the limit

"The sky's the limit" is an inspiring idiom used to convey the idea that there are endless possibilities or opportunities available to someone. We use it when referring to a situation where there are no constraints or boundaries, and one can aim as high as they desire. Its origins can be traced back to the early 20th century when it was used in aviation to describe the notion of unlimited possibilities for aircraft flight. The expression gained popularity during the Space Age, symbolizing humanity's ambition to explore beyond Earth's atmosphere. Over time, it has evolved beyond the aerospace context and is now used widely to encourage others to dream big and reach for their goals without limitations. Today, we use it in various contexts, from career aspirations to personal endeavors, to inspire ourselves and others to aim for greatness.

180. Apple of discord

The phrase "apple of discord" refers to an object of contention or a source of conflict. It originates from Greek mythology, where it was said that Eris, goddess of strife and discord, threw a golden apple into the wedding feast of King Peleus and Thetis, inscribed with the words "For the fairest." This caused a dispute among the goddesses Athena, Aphrodite, and Hera, as each claimed the apple for themselves, leading to the Trojan War. The expression has since been used as a metaphor for something that brings discord and conflict among people.

Did You Know?

Ancient superstitions were beliefs and practices that were not based on scientific or rational explanations. They existed for a variety of reasons, including:

- Fear of the unknown: People in ancient times often feared things they didn't understand, such as natural disasters, illnesses, and death. They created superstitions as a way to try to control or make sense of these unknowns.
- Cultural beliefs: Ancient civilizations often had their own unique belief systems and myths that were passed down from generation to generation. Some of these beliefs became ingrained in their culture as superstitions.
- Religion: Religion was an important part of daily life in ancient times and many superstitions were tied to religious beliefs and rituals. People believed that certain actions or behaviors could please or displease the gods and affect their daily lives.
- Social influence: Superstitions could also be spread and perpetuated through social influence and peer pressure. People may have followed certain beliefs or practices because they felt that others expected it of them.

Examples of ancient superstitions include:

- Throwing salt over one's shoulder to ward off bad luck
- Believing that the number thirteen was unlucky
- Knocking on wood to prevent bad luck
- Carrying a rabbit's foot for good luck
- Believing that eclipses were caused by a dragon or monster eating the sun or moon.

These superstitions may seem absurd or silly today, but they were an important part of daily life in ancient times and helped people to feel a sense of control and comfort in an uncertain world.

181. Bury your head under in the sand

The idiom "bury one's head in the sand" describes a situation in which someone is avoiding facing a problem or reality by pretending it does not exist. The phrase implies that the person is trying to avoid dealing with the problem by ignoring it and hoping it will go away. It is often used to describe people who are in denial about something or who are unwilling to take responsibility for a situation. The expression is thought to have originated from the behavior of ostriches, which are known to bury their heads in sand when they feel threatened. However, the belief that ostriches bury their heads in the sand to avoid danger is a myth, but it probably inspired the phrase nonetheless.

182. Have a beef

The idiom "have a beef" is an American expression that means to have a complaint or a grievance, to have a problem with something or someone, or to have a reason to be upset. The phrase "have a beef" originated in the early 20th century and was initially used in the context of the meatpacking industry. Beef was one of the main products of the meatpacking industry, and the phrase "have a beef" referred to having a complaint or grievance about the quality of the beef being produced. As the term became popular among the workers in the meatpacking industry, it gradually spread to other industries and eventually entered the everyday language.

183. Bite off more than you can chew

To "bite off more than you can chew" means to take on more than one can handle or to attempt something that is beyond one's ability. There are two different theories about the origins of this idiom. One theory is that it comes from the idea of literally trying to bite off more food than one can comfortably chew and swallow. The second theory is that it comes from the idea of taking on more work or responsibilities than one can handle, similar to the metaphor of having "too much on one's plate."

184. Sleep on it

"To sleep on it" is a well-established idiomatic expression that has been in use since the 1500s. It is a common phrase that is used to convey the idea of taking time to reflect and consider a decision or course of action before making a final choice. The earliest recorded use of this phrase can be found in the *State Papers* of Henry VIII, where it is recorded that "His grace said: '… the world slepe an dreme upon the matter.'" This phrase is based on the idea that when one sleeps, the mind is able to process information and gain a clearer perspective, leading to better decision-making.

185. Get the ball rolling

The phrase "get the ball rolling" means to start something, especially a process or activity, in motion. The origins of this idiom can be traced back to two different sources. The expression "keep the ball rolling" is said to have originated from croquet, which was popularized in Britain in the mid-1850s. Another theory credits America with bringing the phrase into common usage, starting in the 1840s during William Henry Harrison's presidential campaign. Harrison used "Victory Balls," which were ten-foot-diameter leather and tin balls that were pushed from rally to rally while the crowd chanted "Keep the ball rolling." This saying suggests that once momentum is gained, it should be maintained and not allowed to come to a halt. It is often used when starting a new venture, implying that one should not wait for things to happen but should take the initiative to get things moving.

186. Time flies when you're having fun

"Time flies when you're having fun" is a delightful phrase used to express the feeling that time seems to pass quickly when engaged in enjoyable activities. We use it when referring to moments of joy or excitement that seem to make time go by faster than usual. Its origins can be traced back to ancient times, with variations of the idiom appearing in ancient Greek and Latin texts. The expression became more prevalent in the English language during the 19th century, gaining popularity as people recognized the phenomenon of losing track of time during enjoyable experiences. Over time, it has evolved into a well-known saying, often used in conversations, social gatherings, and everyday life to reflect on enjoyable moments and the fleeting nature of time. Today, we use it as a reminder to cherish and savor the moments of happiness that make life memorable and meaningful.

187. Speak of the devil

To "speak of the devil" is an expression used when someone unexpectedly appears during a conversation, after they were just being spoken or thought about. This phrase is often used to express surprise and the coincidence of their sudden appearance. Nowadays, the idiom is fairly innocuous but its origins can be traced back to the Middle Ages in England, where it was used as a cautionary warning against mentioning the devil, Satan, by name. It was believed that speaking about the devil would summon him. In the 1600s, an alternate phrase "talk of the devil" began to be used instead of "speak of the devil." This term originated from two popular sayings "Talk of the Devil and he's presently at your elbow" and "Talk of the Devil and see his horns," which both convey the idea that speaking about the devil would summon his presence and he would appear nearby.

188. Brain drain

The term "brain drain" refers to the loss of highly educated or skilled individuals from a particular place or field, particularly in situations where this loss is seen as detrimental to the field in question. It originated in the United Kingdom in the 1950s. The phrase comes from the idea of a drain being a device that is used to remove water or other liquids from a particular area. It's often used in a negative or critical way, implying that the loss of these individuals is causing problems or hindering progress. However, it can also be used more generally to describe any situation in which skilled individuals are leaving a particular industry.

189. Taste of your own medicine

The idiom "a taste of your own medicine" refers to the act of experiencing the same thing that you have inflicted on others. The phrase is often used in a negative context, suggesting that the person is experiencing something unpleasant that they may have previously wished on another person. This expression can be traced back to a tale narrated by the ancient Greek storyteller Aesop, who lived during the 6th century BC. The story in question, entitled "The Cobbler Turned Doctor," involves a cobbler who creates a remedy that he claims has the capacity to cure any type of poison. When the mayor of a town decides to test the cobbler by asking him to consume poison and then take a dose of his own medicine, the cobbler confesses his deception. The moral of the story is a cautionary one, warning against the dangers of seeking advice from those who lack proper training or expertise in a particular field.

190. Two can play at that game

The idiom "two can play at that game" expresses the idea that if an individual is attempting to gain an advantage or utilize a particular strategy, another individual can also employ the same strategy or tactic. This phrase is frequently employed as a response to situations where an aggressive or unfair action has been taken and serves to convey that the speaker will not be intimidated or outmaneuvered and is willing to engage in the same actions. It most likely originated in the 20th century and the earliest recorded usage of the phrase in print is documented in the late 1920s. The expression has its origins in the realm of gambling or betting, where the idea of "two can play at that game" may have been used to convey that a bet or gamble can be made by more than one person and that one person's action does not have a monopoly on the situation.

Did You Know?

Here are some significant periods in world history:

- The Renaissance (14th - 17th centuries) - A cultural and intellectual revival in Europe characterized by a renewed interest in art, science, and classical learning.
- The Enlightenment (17th - 18th centuries) - A philosophical movement characterized by a focus on reason, science, and individual rights.
- Victorian Era (1837 - 1901) - The Victorian era was a period in British history during the reign of Queen Victoria.
- The Industrial Revolution (18th - 19th centuries) - A period of significant change in which traditional industry was transformed by new inventions and technology, leading to economic and social upheaval.
- The Roaring Twenties (1920s) - A decade of prosperity, cultural change, and social liberation in the aftermath of World War I.
- The Great Depression (1929-1939) - A severe worldwide economic downturn that lasted for a decade and was triggered by the stock market crash of 1929.
- World War II (1939-1945) - A global conflict that involved the majority of the world's nations and resulted in the deaths of millions of people.
- The Cold War (1945-1989) - A geopolitical and ideological conflict between the Western world and the Soviet Union that lasted for several decades.
- The Sixties (1960s) - A decade of social, political, and cultural change, marked by civil rights movements, anti-war protests, and the rise of the counterculture.

Each of these periods had a significant impact on world history and shaped the cultural, political, and social landscape in significant ways.

191. Call a spade a spade

To "call a spade a spade" means to speak candidly or frankly about something, without sugarcoating or attempting to obscure the truth. It is often used to describe someone who is willing to speak their mind and say what they really think, even if it may be difficult or unpleasant to do so. The phrase has its roots in the Greek expression "to call a fig a fig and a trough a trough." It's not certain who first used this term, but it has been attributed to both Aristophanes and Menander. The Greek historian Plutarch also used it in his writings. The original Greek expression is believed to have been vulgar in nature, with "figs" and "troughs" being used as double entendres*. When Erasmus, the classical scholar and humanist, translated the phrase from Greek to Latin, he changed it to "call a spade a spade." This translation, or perhaps more accurately a creative interpretation, became popular due to Erasmus' influence in European intellectual circles. The phrase was then translated into English by Nicholas Udall in 1542 and has been used by many famous authors since, including Charles Dickens and W. Somerset Maugham.

*A double entendre is a figure of speech or a type of wordplay in which a phrase or statement has two meanings, one of which is often risqué or humorous. The phrase can be understood in two ways, one of which is often more innocent or less controversial, while the other is more suggestive or risqué.

192. Throw caution to the wind

The expression "throw caution to the wind" means to act recklessly or to take risks without considering the consequences. It commonly describes a situation where someone acts impulsively or ignores warnings or cautionary advice. There are a few theories about the origin of the phrase. One theory is that it refers to the practice of sailing ships, which were often at the mercy of the wind and had to be navigated carefully. To "throw caution to the wind" in this context would mean to ignore strong winds and sail onward. Another theory is that the phrase is derived from the expression "cast caution aside," which means to disregard caution or to act impulsively. The idiom is often used in a lighthearted or humorous way.

193. Take a toll

The phrase "take a toll" refers to the negative impact or consequences that an event can have. The term is rooted in the historical practice of charging a fee, known as a toll, for the use of a road or bridge. The figurative usage of the expression emerged in the 1800s, although the concept of literally taking a toll dates back centuries. In the past, communities owned bridges and pathways and charged a fee for their use, this fee could be a set amount or a percentage of what the traveler was carrying. The idiom is often used to describe the detrimental effects that a situation can have on an individual or group, where the negative aspects are said to "take a toll" on the participants.

194. Go the extra mile

To "go the extra mile" means to put in more effort or to do more than what is required. It is derived from a biblical passage in the Sermon on the Mount, in which Jesus says: "And whoever compels you to go one mile, go with him two." This verse is taken to mean to go above and beyond what is expected and to exert extra energy in order to accomplish a goal. Today, to say that someone will go the extra mile is a compliment, acknowledging when someone puts forth more effort than is expected.

195. Light at the end of the tunnel

The idiom "light at the end of the tunnel" refers to a sign of hope or improvement in a difficult or seemingly hopeless situation. It is often used to encourage someone to persevere through difficult times, as a reminder that the situation will eventually improve. The origin of this idiom is related to the experience of traveling through a tunnel, where it is dark and one cannot see what is ahead. One of the earliest written uses of this phrase dates back to the late 19th century. It appears in a book called *The Children's Treasury of Virtues* by William Charles Henry Wood, which was published in 1891. The book includes the line, "Hope is the light at the end of the tunnel, and it is a light which never dies."

196. When in doubt, do without

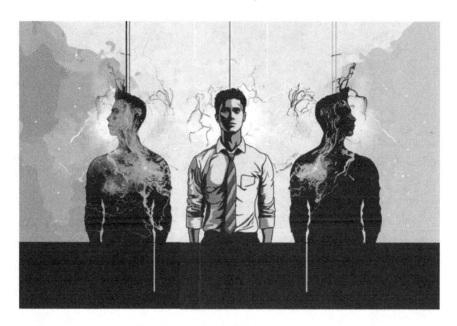

"When in doubt, do without" is a practical idiom advising us to abstain from or avoid something if we are uncertain or unsure about its appropriateness or necessity. We use this expression as a guiding principle when faced with choices or decisions, especially in situations where the consequences of making the wrong choice could be unfavorable. Its origins can be traced back to early English proverbs and similar sentiments found in various cultures worldwide. The phrase gained popularity during the 19th and 20th centuries, as societies embraced frugality and practicality. Over time, its meaning has evolved beyond mere cautionary advice and transformed into a mantra for mindful decision-making. Today, we use it to encourage prudence, reminding ourselves to prioritize thoughtfulness and consideration before indulging in uncertain or unnecessary ventures.

197. Eating out of someone's hand

The idiom "eating out of someone's hand" is used to describe a situation where someone is easily manipulated by another person. The origin of the phrase comes from the idea of training animals, such as dogs or birds, to eat food from a person's hand as a sign of trust and obedience. The expression is usually a metaphor for a relationship where one person has a lot of influence over the other, or where one person is easily swayed by the opinions or actions of another.

198. Talk is cheap

"Talk is cheap" means that actions speak louder than words and that people should be judged by their deeds rather than by what they say. The phrase as it stands today is from the late 19th century and was used to express skepticism about politicians making promises but not following through. The sentiment of this expression can be traced back to 1692, when John Bunyan wrote in his book *The Unsearchable Riches of Christ* that "I know words are cheap, but a dram of grace is worth all the world."

199. Dog and pony show

A "dog and pony show" is used to illustrate a performance or presentation that is designed to be entertaining or impressive, but is ultimately lacking in substance. It originated in the United States in the late 19th century and comes from the idea of a traveling circus or carnival featuring performing animals, such as dogs and ponies. These types of shows were often seen as superficial, with the main attraction being the novelty of the animals rather than any particular skill or talent. Today, the idiom is commonly used in a negative or critical way, implying that a performance is more focused on impressing the audience, rather than providing any real value. It can also be used more generally to describe any situation in which something is being presented in a flashy or impressive manner, but lacks depth.

200. Save something for a rainy day

To "save something for a rainy day" means to set aside something for future use or for a time of need. This expression can be traced back to the mid-16th century in Britain. The phrase is first documented in the play *The Bugbears*, which was translated from Antonio Francesco Grazzini's "La Spirita," and was performed around the year 1561. It is noteworthy that only a single manuscript of the play exists. Additionally, it is of significance to mention that the word "bugbear" in medieval England referred to a hobgoblin depicted as a frightening bear that haunted the woods and scared children. The term "bugbear" is thought to have its roots in the Middle English word "bugge" (a frightening thing) and the old Scots word "bogill" (goblin). In modern times, we might save money, keep an item of clothing, or want to watch a particular movie or show "on a rainy day" in the future.

Did You Know?

Collective nouns are names for a group of things, animals, or people. Here are some funny collective nouns that might make you chuckle:

- A blunder of bureaucrats
- A flamboyance of flamingos
- A prickle of porcupines
- A conspiracy of ravens
- A bask of crocodiles
- A cackle of hyenas
- A mischief of mice
- A gulp of cormorants
- A unkindness of ravens
- A sounder of swine
- A mob of kangaroos
- A school of fish
- An exaltation of larks
- A pace of donkeys
- A parade of peacocks
- A rascal of raccoons
- A skulk of foxes
- A swarm of bees
- An eloquence of skunks
- A tribe of goats

201. Pay lip service

The phrase "pay lip service" originated in the early 20th century as a way to sarcastically remark that someone is giving verbal support for a particular idea or cause, but does not take any meaningful action to support it. The term implies a lack of genuine commitment or follow-through and is often used to criticize or express skepticism about someone's true beliefs. The earliest known written use of the expression is found in a letter dated August 12, 1906, by American lawyer and politician William Jennings Bryan to the American Federation of Labor, where he wrote "The people who pay lip service to the Constitution, but seek to destroy it by judicial construction." It's later found in the 1915 novel, *The Red Planet* by William J. Locke and in a 1917 article of *The Times*, London, where it is used to describe the behavior of certain politicians who "pay lip service to the cause of the labouring classes."

202. Desperate times call for desperate measures

"Desperate times call for desperate measures" is used to convey that when one is in a dire situation, they may need to take extreme actions in order to survive or overcome the situation. The phrase is believed to have originated with a saying coined by the ancient Greek physician, Hippocrates, in his work *Amorphisms*, where he wrote: "For extreme diseases, extreme methods of cure, as to restriction, are most suitable." Nowadays, the expression can be used in a serious context but is often said in a sarcastic way about low-stakes scenario.

203. The grass is always greener

There are a few theories about the origin of "the grass is always greener." It perhaps originated from the practice of comparing one's own lawn or grass to that of a neighbor's. Another theory is that the phrase originated from the practice of grazing livestock. Sheep, cows, and other animals are naturally inclined to move on to greener pastures as soon as the grass they are eating becomes less lush. This behavior led to the idea that the grass is always greener on the other side of the fence. The expression has morphed into the idea that people often compare their own lives to the lives of others and find them wanting. People tend to think that others have it better than they do, whether it's a better job, a better partner, or a better home. The phrase is now widely used to describe the tendency for people to envy or covet what others have and to overlook or underestimate the value of what they already have.

204. Busybody

The term "busybody" refers to a person who is excessively or unnecessarily involved in the affairs of others. It originated in the 16th century and likely comes from the concept of being "busy," which has long been associated with being productive and active. In the context of the idiom, a "busybody" is someone who is constantly poking their nose into other people's business, often without being invited or welcomed. This can be seen as intrusive or annoying, as the person is not minding their own business but rather constantly trying to be involved in the affairs of others. Oftentimes, saying that so-and-so is acting like a "busybody" is a negative way to describe someone who is overly nosy. However, it can also be used in a more lighthearted or playful manner to refer to someone who is simply very curious or interested in the goings-on of those around them.

205. On the same page

The origin of the phrase "on the same page" is a topic of much discussion, with some speculating that it might have come from choral singing. In choral singing, it is essential for all participants to be in harmony and to sing from the same sheet of music. However, it is much more likely that this idiom can be attributed to business and educational settings, where copies of a single document or material are distributed among a group, and all members are required to be reading from the same page in order to effectively understand and discuss the topic at hand. The expression is employed to describe a situation where people are in agreement and working towards a common goal. This phrase has been in use since the early 20th century and it has become popular in the context of business, politics, and other fields where people work together. It implies that everyone is in agreement and that there is a shared understanding of the situation.

206. Let the cat out of the bag

"Let the cat out of the bag" is an idiom that has been in use for centuries. It originated in the 18th century, when markets were a common place for buying and selling goods, including animals. Unscrupulous merchants would often try to deceive buyers by substituting a cat for a piglet and selling it in a bag. If the deception was discovered, they would "let the cat out of the bag," revealing the surprise and ruining the sale. This practice gave rise to the idiomatic expression, which is now used more generally to refer to any situation where a secret or surprise is revealed prematurely. The first literary reference to the phrase can be found in *The London Magazine* in 1760, indicating that the expression was already in common use at that time.

207. Add insult to injury

To "add insult to injury" describes a situation in which someone makes a bad situation even worse by doing or saying something hurtful or offensive. The phrase suggests that an initial problem or injury is being compounded by an additional, often intentional, affront. This term is extremely old, it comes from one of the fables told by Aesop, who lived in Ancient Greece. The story, "The Bald Man and the Fly," is about a bald man who gets bitten on the head by a fly. He attempts to thwart the fly by striking himself on the head, but ends up hurting himself more. The fly then flies away and makes fun of the bald man, saying that if he's willing to hurt himself like that just to get back at an insect, what will he do to himself for insulting himself, too? The point of the story is that revenge only ends up hurting the person seeking it.

208. Pardon my French

"Pardon my French" is an idiomatic expression that is used as a polite or humorous way of apologizing for using profanity or strong language. The phrase is believed to have originated in the 19th century as a reference to the use of profanity in the French language, which was considered more acceptable than in English-speaking cultures. One of the earliest recorded uses of the term was in a story published by Karl Von Miltie in 1831 in his book *The Twelve Nights*, where he writes: "My dear Mr. Heartwell, you are come to see me at last. Bless me, how fat you are grown!—absolutely round as a ball:—you will soon be as embonpoint (excuse my French) as your poor dear father, the major." In this example, Karl is not apologizing for the insult, but rather for using the French word "embonpoint" to describe someone's weight. This illustrates that the phrase can be used not only to apologize for profanity but also for using a foreign language. It can also be employed in a humorous way, to mock the idea that French is a more sophisticated or refined language.

209. Beat the clock

To "beat the clock" means to finish something within a certain time limit or before a deadline. It is commonly used in the context of a race or competition, where the goal is to complete a task faster than one's opponents. The origin of this idiom is thought to be related to the popular television show *Beat the Clock*, which aired in the United States from 1950 to 1958 and was later revived in the 1970s. The show featured a series of challenges or stunts that contestants had to complete within a certain time limit in order to win prizes. The earliest use of the phrase outside of the show dates back to 1952, in an article published in the *Chicago Daily Tribune*. The article mentions the television show *Beat the Clock* and refers to the expression as a "catchphrase."

210. In your element

When someone tells you that you're "in your element," it means you are comfortable in your surroundings. The expression came from the Victorian era, where all things were classified as belonging to one of the four elements; earth, fire, air, and water. The idiom means someone is in a situation where they can use their skills, abilities, or interests to their full potential. It suggests that the person is comfortable and confident in their surroundings and is able to excel or perform at a high level. The origins of this phrase are somewhat unclear, but it is thought to have come from the ancient Greek philosopher and scientist Aristotle, who believed that everything in the universe had a natural place or "element" where it belonged and functioned best. Today, the expression is used more figuratively to describe someone who is comfortable and confident in a particular situation or environment and is able to excel or perform at a high level. It is often used to express admiration or respect for someone who is particularly skilled or talented.

Did You Know?

The longest hiccups on record lasted sixty-eight years.

Humans are the only animals that produce tears when they cry.

The human body contains enough fat to make seven bars of soap.

The Great Barrier Reef, the world's largest coral reef system, is visible from space and is so large that it can be seen with the naked eye.

There is a type of jellyfish called the immortal jellyfish (Turritopsis dohrnii) that is capable of reversing its life cycle and becoming a juvenile again after it reaches sexual maturity. This means that it has the potential to live forever, as long as it is not eaten by a predator or subjected to other forms of mortality.

211. Pull strings

The expression "to pull strings" means to use one's influence or connections to get something done. The phrase originated in the late 1800s and comes from the idea of manipulating the strings of a puppet to make it move. In this context, pulling strings refers to controlling someone or something to achieve a desired outcome. The idiom is commonly used to express influence or connections in a political or business context, as it implies that someone is using their power or resources to get things done in a secretive or underhanded way. The term is also used to describe people who use their connections to gain an advantage in their personal life.

212. Blow hot and cold

The idiom "blow hot and cold" refers to a situation in which someone is inconsistent in their behavior or opinions. It's thought to be derived from the ancient Greek philosopher Aristotle's observation that people with fevers would often alternately feel extremely hot and very cold. In this context, the phrase referred to the idea of fluctuating between two extreme states or conditions. In modern times, the expression is used more broadly to refer to any situation in which someone is indecisive in their behavior or opinions, and can be applied to a wide range of situations, including relationships, career decisions, and other areas of life.

213. To have sticky fingers

The idiom "to have sticky fingers" means to have a tendency to steal or take things that do not belong to you. It is often used to describe someone who is dishonest or prone to stealing. There are three different theories about the origins and history of the idiom. The first theory refers to the way in which thieves might use their fingers to take small items without being noticed, leaving behind a sticky residue on the stolen item. The second theory is that it may be a reference to the way in which people with a sweet tooth might get a sticky residue on their fingers when eating candy or other sweets. The third suggests it may have originated in the gold mining industry, where workers used sap or honey on their fingers to collect gold dust and then pocketed the value of the gold when it was weighed for payment. Nowadays, the phrase can be used in a serious manner when referring to criminals, or in a mild manner like referring to a child who frequently takes others' toys.

The phrase "pull a Houdini" refers to someone who is able to escape from a difficult situation or confinement. The expression is derived from the name of the famous magician and escape artist, Harry Houdini, who was known for his death-defying stunts and ability to escape from seemingly impossible situations. Houdini began his career as a magician in the late 19th century, and quickly became famous for his spectacular illusions and escapes. He would often perform stunts where he would escape from handcuffs, straitjackets, and even from sealed containers such as milk cans and packing crates. He was also known for his ability to escape from prison cells and other confinement. The phrase "pull a Houdini" first appeared in print in the early 20th century. A fun fact about the magician and escape artist Harry Houdini is that he was a skilled aviator. Houdini purchased one of the first airplanes in America and taught himself how to fly it. He even performed aerial stunts and tricks as part of his magic act.

215. Toot your own horn

The expression "toot your own horn" means to boast or speak proudly about one's accomplishments, skills, or achievements. We use it when someone is openly praising themselves or drawing attention to their positive qualities. The phrase likely originated from the act of musicians blowing their own horns to get noticed during a performance, which symbolizes self-promotion. While its exact first use in writing is unclear, the idiom's concept has been present in various cultures for centuries. Over time, its meaning has evolved to encompass not only musical talents but any form of self-promotion or bragging. Today, we use "toot your own horn" both playfully and critically, reminding each other to be humble and let our accomplishments speak for themselves, rather than boasting excessively.

216. On a shoestring

The idiom "on a shoestring" is used to describe a situation where resources are limited and tight budgets are involved. The exact origins of the phrase are not entirely clear, however, it has been in use since at least the 1800s. One theory suggests that the phrase originated from the idea of a shoestring being thin and not very strong, and therefore, not able to support much weight. The metaphor is that if one is living on a shoestring, they are living with very limited resources and are not able to afford much. Another theory suggests that the idiom may have originated from gambling game "faro," where a "shoestring gambler" referred to a petty, tinhorn gambler who only had limited resources to gamble with. In modern context, if a household is on a "shoestring budget" then the family is struggling to make ends meet and might need to take actions like cutting expenses, working extra, shopping thrifty, and other methods in order to save money.

217. Easier said than done

The phrase "easier said than done" means that a task or action may sound simple or straightforward when discussed or suggested, but it is actually much more challenging or complicated to accomplish in reality. We use this expression to convey that verbalizing a plan or solution is far less demanding than the actual implementation. The origins of this idiom can be traced back to ancient proverbs and sayings that highlight the gap between words and actions. While its exact first use in writing remains unclear, similar phrases have appeared in various cultures throughout history. Its meaning has remained consistent over time, emphasizing the difficulty of translating ideas into practical actions. Nowadays, we use it to acknowledge the complexities and obstacles involved in turning intentions into achievements, serving as a gentle reminder to approach tasks with a sense of realism and determination.

218. Doggy bag

A "doggy bag" or "doggie bag" refers to the container of leftover food that one might take home from a restaurant. The origin of the phrase comes from the practice of people taking home leftovers for their pets, specifically dogs, which is where it gets its name. The expression is thought to have originated in the United States in the 1940s, during World War II, as a way to reduce food waste. It is believed that it first started at various restaurants across the nation, with some providing waxed paper bags for customers to take home leftovers for their dogs. Another story claims it originated in a New York restaurant called *Dan Stampler's Steak Joint* in 1949, where the owner created a bag with a picture of his Scottish terrier on it and called it a doggie bag.

219. A sandwich short of a picnic

The phrase "a sandwich short of a picnic" is used to refer to someone who is a little eccentric or is not quite right in the head. The expression suggests that the person is missing something essential, just like a sandwich is an essential component of a picnic, but not having one doesn't make a picnic incomplete. The origins of this idiom are fairly recent, the first documented use of it is from the BBC's Lenny Henry Christmas Special, December 1987. It's likely that the phrase was created by the writer as a humorous way to describe someone who is a bit scatterbrained or disoriented. It's commonly used in a light-hearted way, and it's not meant to be taken seriously or as an insult.

220. Right off the bat

The idiom "right off the bat" means immediately or without delay and hesitation. It originated from the American game of baseball, where it is used to describe a well-struck ball. The term was first used in the 1880s, with both literal and figurative usage. It is primarily used in North America, although some believe there may be a link to the game of cricket as well. The earliest written use of this phrase dates back to the early 20th century in a book called *The American Language* by H.L. Mencken, which was published in 1919.

Did You Know?

The shortest war in history was between Britain and Zanzibar on August 27, 1896. The conflict lasted just thirty-eight minutes, with the British side quickly gaining control of the East African island-state. This brief conflict marked the end of the Sultanate of Zanzibar and the start of British rule, which lasted until 1964.

The tallest person in history was Robert Wadlow, who was 8 feet 11 inches (2.71 meters) tall.

The highest mountain in the solar system is Olympus Mons, which is located on Mars. It is approximately three times higher than Mount Everest and is the largest volcano in the solar system.

The oldest known tree in the world is a bristlecone pine tree in California's White Mountains. It is over five thousand years old and is still alive.

The longest animal in the world is the lion's mane jellyfish, which can grow up to 120 feet (36.57 meters) in length.

The world's largest snowflake on record was reported to have fallen in Montana in 1887. It was fifteen inches wide and eight inches thick (thirty-eight centimeters wide and twenty centimeters thick).

221. On thin ice

The expression "on thin ice" refers to a situation in which someone is in a vulnerable or precarious position. It is thought to have originated in the 16th century and is likely derived from the idea of walking on thin ice, which can be dangerous because it is prone to breaking. It can be used to describe a wide range of situations, including in casual conversation, in written media, or in other forms of communication. The phrase is a common idiom in English and is often used to convey a sense of risk or danger.

222. Smell a rat

The idiom "to smell a rat" means to suspect that something is wrong or that someone is hiding a secret. It is frequently used to express suspicion or distrust of a situation or person. The origin of this phrase is believed to come from the old English saying "to smell rat," which was used to describe the ability of a rat-catcher's dog to detect the presence of rats. The expression was first used in the 1500s to describe the dog's sense of smell to detect rats, then it passed on to be used metaphorically to refer to the ability of humans to sense when something is not right.

223. Low man on the totem pole

The expression "low man on the totem pole" is a colloquialism that pertains to an individual occupying the lowest rank within a hierarchy or organization, often characterized by a lack of power or authority. This phrase is frequently used to describe a newcomer to a job or organization, or an individual who is not held in high esteem. It originated from North American indigenous cultures, specifically from the totem poles found in many tribes. Totem poles are wooden sculptures that depict the tribe's history, legends, and spiritual beliefs, with figures arranged in a hierarchical order, with the most significant figures at the top and the less significant figures at the bottom. The phrase was first used in the early 20th century and was coined by Fred Allen, an American comedian, in the 1940s.

224. Up in arms

"Up in arms" has been in use since the 16th century and originally referred to a physical posture in which a person held their arms up in a defensive or aggressive position, often in preparation for battle. The phrase has evolved over time to take on a more figurative meaning, and is now commonly used to refer to a situation in which a group of people are strongly and actively protesting or opposing something. The exact origin of the expression is uncertain, but it likely developed from the literal practice of soldiers raising their weapons in preparation for combat. The phrase has been used in a variety of contexts over the centuries, including in political and social protests, and is now a common idiom in English. In modern usage, it typically refers to a situation in which a group of people are strongly and actively opposing or protesting against something.

225. Full of beans

"Full of beans" is a colloquial phrase that is used to express the state of being lively, energetic, and enthusiastic. It is often used to describe someone who is in a good mood, talkative, or active. The origins of this expression are not entirely clear, but it is believed to have emerged in Europe in the 14th century. According to one theory, the idiom has its origins in the practice of feeding horses exclusively with beans grown for animal feed. The consumption of these beans was observed to result in a noticeable increase in the horses' liveliness and energy, leading to the coining of the phrase to describe this state of vivacity. Another theory is that it comes from the saying "full of life," which has a similar meaning. Additionally, the phrase "full of pep" also carries a similar connotation. It is worth noting that this idiom is not limited to describing positive characteristics, it can also be used in a negative sense to refer to someone who is overly talkative or excessively active, especially when it is seen as annoying or unwanted.

"Playing by ear" is a phrase that refers to a musician's ability to play a piece of music without the need for sheet music. This means that the musician is able to listen to a piece of music, and then replicate it on their instrument without the need for written notation. This skill is often associated with pianists and keyboard players, but it can also apply to other instruments such as guitar, drums, and even singing. The origins of the expression date back to the 18th century, when musicians were primarily self-taught. In this era, written music was not as widely available as it is today, and many musicians had to rely on their own ability to replicate what they heard. Over time, the idiom "play by ear" has come to be used more broadly to mean improvising or going with the flow without a specific plan or script.

227. Crème de la crème

The idiom "crème de la crème" is a French phrase that literally means "cream of the cream" and is used to describe the best of the best, the elite, or the top of a group or class. The origin of this expression is thought to come from the culinary world, where it was used to refer to the finest and most expensive ingredients, like the cream that rises to the top of the milk. The idiom originated in France, where items like cream and cheese have been popular for centuries and are considered symbols of elegance and exclusivity. People who had cream or cream-based desserts in their homes would have been considered wealthy.

228. An eye for an eye

"An eye for an eye" is a principle of retaliation in which the punishment inflicted on an offender is equivalent to the harm suffered by the victim. It is frequently used to refer to the idea of seeking revenge or retribution for a wrongdoing. The phrase comes from ancient Mesopotamian and Hebrew cultures, and is found in the Code of Hammurabi and the Hebrew Bible, both dating back to around 1750 BC. The principle of "an eye for an eye" was intended to limit retaliation and ensure that the punishment fit the crime, rather than allowing for excessive or arbitrary punishment. This concept was later adopted by other ancient cultures, such as the Greeks and Romans, and has been a part of legal systems and cultures around the world.

229. Stick one's neck out

The expression "stick one's neck out" describes taking a risk or making a bold move, often in a situation where there is a potential for failure or negative consequences. The phrase is derived from the image of a turtle or other animal sticking its neck out of its shell, which would be a vulnerable position as it exposes its neck to attack. By extension, the idiom is used to refer to someone who is taking a risk or putting themselves in a potentially dangerous or vulnerable position by speaking out or taking action. Another idea suggests that the phrase may have originated as American slang some sixty years ago, based on the backyard chicken that was laid on a chopping block with its neck stretched out, ready to be beheaded with an ax. This theory suggests that the saying means to take a risk and expose oneself to criticism, which is closely related to an older form of the phrase that can be found in Shakespeare's play *Henry V*, where Fluellen says, "Let his neck answer for it."

230. Touch base

The phrase "touch base" is used to describe the act of making contact or having a brief conversation with someone, usually for the purpose of catching up or checking in. This terminology comes from the world of sports, specifically baseball in America. In baseball, touching bases as a batter rounds the infield is necessary in order to advance. The expression was adopted into everyday language in the 1930s and is one of many baseball-related idioms that have been incorporated into everyday language. For example, "getting to first base" means to make a positive start, "off base" means to be mistaken or wide of the mark, and "touching all the bases" means to have everything covered and implies success, similar to hitting a home run and touching all the bases in a victory circuit.

Did You Know?

The Great Wall of China is a series of fortifications made of brick, tamped earth, stone, and other materials, generally built along an east-to-west line across the northern borders of China to protect against the raids and invasions of various nomadic tribes throughout China's history. It is the longest wall in the world, stretching over thirteen thousand miles (20,900 kilometers) and is a UNESCO World Heritage Site.

A blue whale is the largest animal on earth and its heart is accordingly massive. In fact, a blue whale's heart is so big that a human could swim through its arteries. It can weigh up to a thousand pounds (454 kilograms) and is around the size of a small car.

The Empire State Building is a world-famous skyscraper located in New York City. It was completed in just one year and forty-five days, with construction starting on March 17, 1930, and the building opening to the public on May 1, 1931. At the time of its completion, it was the tallest building in the world, a title it held for forty years.

A group of flamingos is called a "flamboyance." This term refers to the birds' striking appearance and graceful movements, and is used to describe a gathering of these distinctive, wading birds. Flamingos are known for their long, thin legs and distinctive pink coloration, which comes from the pigments in the algae and small crustaceans that make up their diet.

231. New ground

The expression "new ground" or "to break new ground" is a phrase that has been in use for centuries. It originates from the literal act of breaking new ground in agriculture or construction, where new land is being cleared or worked on for the first time. The term has been used throughout history in diverse areas, including mining, excavating, farming, archaeology, arboriculture, and even animal training. The idiom has become popularized in its current context due to its versatility and wide range of usage. It implies that something is different, innovative, or original, and it could also imply that the new thing being done is taking a new direction or is a first-time attempt.

232. Hold the fort

The phrase "hold the fort" originated in the United States during the 1800s along the American Frontier. The expression is thought to have come from the military, where soldiers were ordered to hold a fort or stronghold against an enemy attack, and it was used as a call to action, urging people to defend their position and not to give up. One example of the origin is traced to an order given by General William Tecumseh Sherman in 1864, which was repeated as, "Hold the fort [against the enemy at Allatoona] at all costs, for I am coming." This phrase was used as a battle cry to remind them of their duty and to not give up.

"At face value" means to accept something as it appears without questioning or examining it further. The phrase suggests that the person is looking only at the surface or exterior of something, rather than examining it more deeply. It is commonly used to describe someone who is too trusting or gullible, and who is not skeptical or critical enough when evaluating information. The term "face value" has been used literally since the 1870s to refer to the monetary value printed on a bank note, stock certificate, bond, or ticket. These items may often sell at prices that are higher than the valuation written on them. But, if an item is sold for the amount of money printed on its face, it is said to be sold at face value. The term has been used figuratively since the late 1800s.

234. Swan song

The term "swan song" refers to a final performance or appearance, especially one that is considered to be the best or most memorable. It is frequently used to describe an artist's final work or an athlete's final game. The origins of this idiom can be traced back to the ancient Greek myth of the swan, which was said to sing a beautiful song just before it died. The myth of the swan song was first recorded in the works of the Greek playwright Aeschylus in his play *Agamemnon*, which was written in 458 BC. In the play, Cassandra sings a death-laden lament like a swan before she dies. The myth of the swan song is a well-known motif that was popularized by the Romans and extensively utilized in literature and visual art. The legend states that swans maintain a characteristic silence throughout their lives, only to produce a melodious, final song upon their imminent death. However, it is important to note that this is a misconception, as swans are actually quite vocal creatures and are not known for singing melodic songs.

235. Heart misses a beat

The idiom "heart misses a beat" means to experience a sudden feeling of excitement or surprise. The origin of this saying is related to the physical sensation of the heart skipping a beat or pausing briefly in response to some sort of stimulation or excitement. The earliest written use of this phrase dates back to the early 20th century. It appears in a book called *The American Language* by H.L. Mencken, which was published in 1919. The book includes the line, "To have one's heart miss a beat is to experience a sudden feeling of excitement or surprise."

236. Feel like death warmed up

To "look or feel like death warmed up" is used to describe a person who looks or feels very sick or unwell. It first came about in the United Kingdom in the early 20th century. One theory is that it comes from the idea of death being personified as a cold or pale figure, and that the act of "warming up" death would involve bringing it back to life or giving it some color. Another theory is that it may have originated as a way of describing the appearance of someone who has been ill or has not been taking care of themselves. Nowadays, it's used in a lighthearted or playful manner, implying that the person is not actually on the brink of death but simply looks very ill.

237. Fair dinkum

The phrase "fair dinkum" originated in Australia in the late 19th century. It is derived from the word "dinkum," which is a slang term that has two meanings: "work" and "fair play." The term "dinkum" originated as "honest toil" and was used to refer to hardworking, honest labor. The expression "fair dinkum" is a combination of the word "dinkum" and the adjective "fair," which means "just" or "true." This idiom is used to indicate that something is true or genuine, and also to express agreement.

238. Fish out of water

The idiom "fish out of water" refers to someone who is feeling uncomfortable or out of place in a particular situation or environment. This phrase suggests the idea of a fish being removed from its natural habitat, where it is able to swim and thrive, and placed in an unfamiliar setting where it is unable to function as it normally would. This idiom has a long history, with the first recorded use of it appearing in the work of English writer Geoffrey Chaucer in the year 1483. In his famous book, *The Canterbury Tales*, Chaucer used this expression to describe a character who was struggling to ride a horse and felt uneasy in this new and unfamiliar situation: "... A huge man, uncouth; a master of vessel and knew all the ports; not ride well; like a fish out of water as sat on his horse."

239. Rings a bell

The expression "rings a bell" means to seem familiar or to remind one of something. It is often used when someone cannot quite remember or place something, but it is familiar in some way. There are a few theories about the origins of this idiom, including the idea that it may be a reference to the ringing of a bell to signal the start or end of an event, or to the bell that is rung to signify the start or end of a round in a boxing match. One proposed explanation for the origin of this idiomatic expression is its association with the research of Ivan Pavlov, a late 19th and early 20th century Russian physiologist and neurologist. In his groundbreaking study, Pavlov demonstrated the phenomenon of classical conditioning in dogs through the use of a ringing bell as a conditioned stimulus. The dogs, having consistently received food in conjunction with the sound of the bell, eventually exhibited a conditioned response of salivation at the mere auditory cue of the bell, anticipating the presentation of food.

240. Get out of hand

To "get out of hand" means to become difficult to control or manage. It is often used to refer to a situation or event that has become chaotic or unmanageable. The phrase is thought to have originated in the early 20th century and it's likely derived from the idea of trying to hold onto something and losing control of it. The expression comes from the concept of losing control of a horse when riding a team of horses pulling a wagon. If the rider lets go of the reins or does not keep a firm grip, then they cannot control the horses. Hence, the horses will be "out of hand."

Did You Know?

A sneeze can travel up to a hundred miles (160 kilometres) per hour and can spread germs up to twenty feet (six meters) away.

A single teaspoon of a neutron star would weigh about six billion tons.

A cat has the ability to always land on its feet thanks to a flexible spine and an inner ear that helps it sense which way is up.

The average person spends six months of their life waiting for red lights to turn green.

The Nile is the longest river in the world, stretching over four thousand miles (6,437 kilometers) from its source in Burundi to its mouth in Egypt. The river has been a vital source of water and transportation for the people of Egypt for thousands of years and played a key role in the development of ancient Egyptian civilization. The Nile remains an important economic resource for the countries through which it flows, providing water for agriculture, industry, and human consumption.

The air you exhale contains enough carbon dioxide to kill a person if it were all concentrated in one place. This is because carbon dioxide is toxic in high concentrations. Normal levels of carbon dioxide in the air we breathe are harmless, but if the concentration becomes too high, it can interfere with oxygen uptake in the lungs and lead to suffocation. This is why miners and underwater divers often use breathing apparatus that filters out excess carbon dioxide to keep air supply safe.

241. Go back to the drawing board

The idiom "go back to the drawing board" means to start something again from the beginning or to go back to the planning stage. It is mainly used in the context of business or engineering, when a project or product is not successful and needs to be redesigned or reevaluated. The origin of this idiom is thought to come from the practice of using a drawing board in design and engineering. A drawing board is a large, flat surface used to make and modify technical drawings. When a project or product is not successful, designers or engineers might have to go back to the drawing board and start again from the beginning, redesigning and reevaluating their plans. The phrase was first seen in a cartoon by the US cartoonist Peter Arno, which was published in *The New Yorker* in 1941. The cartoon shows a smoldering airplane that has just crashed and a designer is walking away saying, "Well, back to the old drawing board."

242. Sleep with the fishes

To "sleep with the fishes" is a phrase that is used to refer to death, particularly murder. It may have been used by the Mafia and other criminal organizations to describe disposing of someone's body by throwing it in the ocean, where it would "sleep with the fishes." This expression was popularized by movies and TV shows that depicted the American Mafia, such as *The Godfather* and *The Sopranos*. However, the origin of the idiom may go back much farther. According to some theories, the phrase was used by Edmund Spencer in the 1830s in *Sketches of Germany and the Germans*, where he described a trip by a British angler to an area occupied by superstitious villagers who considered fly fishing a form of black magic. Spencer wrote: "This terrible apprehension was soon circulated from village to village: the deluded peasants broke in pieces the pretty painted magic wand, and forcibly put to flight the magician himself, vowing, with imprecations, if he repeated his visit, they would send him to sleep with the fishes." Even in Homer's *The Iliad*, there is a passage, "Make your bed with the fishes now…"

243. Skid row

"Skid row" is a term used to describe a run-down and poor neighborhood in a city. It's often where homeless people or people who move around a lot live. The phrase started in the late 1800s when loggers would set up camp near the "skid road" where they slid logs to the sawmill or river. Over time, the areas became known as "skid row." During the Great Depression, many people lost their jobs and became homeless. This led to the creation of skid row areas in cities all over the US. These places were known for having a lot of homeless people and cheap places to stay. They were often poor, had crime, and made people feel hopeless. Today, skid row areas still exist in many US cities, with an area in downtown Los Angeles functionally termed Skid Row. The term "skid row" has also come to describe communities of people who struggle with addiction or mental health problems. People are trying to make these areas better by improving housing and offering more help to those in need.

244. Hard pill to swallow

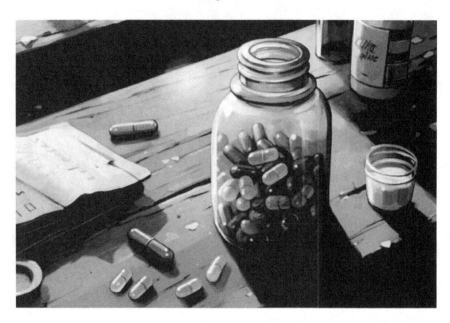

A "hard pill to swallow" is used to describe something that is difficult to accept or believe, or that is painful to endure. It is one variant of an idiom that has been in use for hundreds of years. The expression first appeared in the 1600s as a "pill to swallow" and, at the time, a pill was considered a foul thing to ingest. The variation "a bitter pill to swallow" came into use in the 1700s, and the final expression, "a hard pill to swallow," came into use in the 1800s. Nowadays, the phrase "a bitter pill to swallow" is about twice as popular as the term "a hard pill to swallow." This expression in its current form started appearing in written work, with the earliest use of this idiom found in the *Morning Journal* newspaper from 1829: "That they will prove a hard pill for Turkey to swallow is to be expected, unless, indeed, some decided friend has recently sprung up, who will not allow Turkey to be so crippled as to make her fall an easy prey next time she is attacked."

245. No brainer

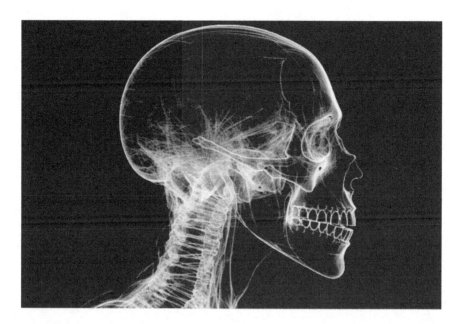

The term "no brainer" is used to describe a decision that is very easy to make or a situation that is readily resolved. It originated in the United States in the 1970s and comes from the idea of using one's brain to make decisions or solve problems. The phrase suggests that the decision or situation in question is so obvious or straightforward that it requires little or no thought or effort to make or resolve. Today, it's used in a casual or lighthearted manner, implying that the decision or situation is not particularly important or significant.

246. Chip off the old block

The expression "chip off the old block" refers to a person who closely resembles their parent or other family member in terms of their appearance, personality, or other characteristics. It originated in the 19th century and is likely derived from the idea of carving a small piece or "chip" from a larger block of wood or stone in order to create a new piece that closely resembles the original. Today, the phrase is used to convey a sense of similarity, with the implication that the offspring is just like the parent.

247. Stuck in a rut

To be "stuck in a rut" means that someone is trapped in a situation where they cannot make progress or change. They could feel confined or unfulfilled and may be experiencing a lack of motivation or a sense of stagnation. The idiom goes back to the 1800s when wagons would get stuck in the trenches created by other wagons' wheels on frequently-traveled roads. If one wagon needed to veer off the road, they would frequently find themselves stuck. Nowadays, "stuck in a rut" is often used to refer to someone feeling trapped in a repetitive or unfulfilling situation and unable to make progress.

248. Knee jerk reaction

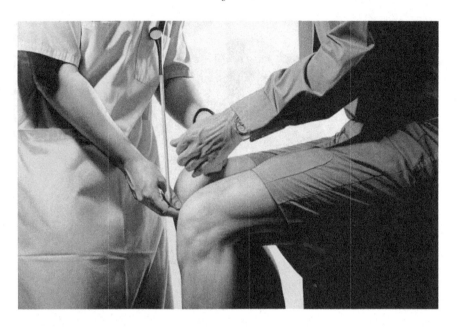

A "knee-jerk reaction" refers to a rapid, automatic, and often emotional response, without careful consideration or thought. It often describes a response that is based on habit, instinct, or preconceived notions, rather than on logical analysis or critical thinking. The origin of this idiom is related to the reflexive action of the knee when the patellar tendon is tapped. When the patellar tendon is tapped, the knee reflexively jerks or kicks outward. This reflex is a simple and automatic response that is controlled by the spinal cord and does not involve conscious thought. The earliest written use of this phrase dates back to the early 20th century. It appears in a book called *Psychology and Life* by Robert S. Woodworth, which was published in 1918. The book defines the term as "a reflex action of the knee caused by a tap on the patellar tendon, and also used to describe a quick and automatic response to something, without careful consideration."

249. Shot across the bow

The phrase "shot across the bow" means a warning or cautionary message. It comes from the naval practice of firing a warning shot across the bow of another ship as a signal to stop or change course. This was a way to avoid a more serious confrontation or conflict at sea. In modern usage, the expression is commonly used to refer to any warning or cautionary message that is meant to prevent a situation from escalating. It can be used in a variety of contexts, such as in business or politics, to signal that further, more serious, action may be taken if necessary.

250. Ground zero

The term "ground zero" is an idiomatic expression that refers to the point of origin or the center of an event or activity, often used in reference to a catastrophic event such as a nuclear explosion, terrorist attack, or natural disaster. The phrase originated in the early 20th century, specifically in reference to the point on the ground directly beneath the point of detonation of a nuclear bomb. The term "ground zero" first came into use on September 4, 1945, in a *New York Times* report on the atomic bombing of Nagasaki, Japan. It was used to describe the location of the bomb's detonation and the area of the most severe damage. It was later used in reference to the point of origin of other catastrophic events, such as the September 11, 2011, terrorist attacks on the World Trade Center in New York City.

Did You Know?

Humans share fifty percent of their DNA with bananas. This fact is due to the similarities in the genetic code of all living things. While it may seem surprising, it's actually a result of the fact that all living things share a common ancestry and have evolved from a single, ancestral organism over billions of years. The similarities in genetic code between species can reveal important information about the relationships between species and the evolutionary processes that have shaped the diversity of life on Earth.

A hummingbird is capable of hovering in midair by flapping its wings at rates of up to eighty beats per second. This remarkable feat of flight is possible due to the high wing-flapping frequency, which generates lift and allows the bird to remain stationary in midair. Hummingbirds are also able to fly forwards, backwards, and even upside down, making them one of the most agile birds in the world.

The human nose can detect over one trillion different scents, making it one of the most advanced sensory organs in the animal kingdom. This incredible ability to distinguish between different scents is due to the complex structure of the olfactory system in the human nose, which contains over four hundred different types of odor receptors. These receptors allow us to detect a wide range of different scents, from the pleasing aroma of freshly baked bread to the unpleasant odor of a skunk. The ability to detect and distinguish between different scents is critical to our survival, as it helps us to identify potential dangers and locate food.

251. Packed like sardines

The expression "packed like sardines" describes a situation where people or objects are crowded together in a tight or cramped space. It originated in the early 20th century and comes from the practice of packing sardines in cans. Sardines are small fish that are often packed tightly, one on top of the other, in order to conserve space and make them easier to transport. The image of sardines packed closely together in a can is used as a metaphor for people or objects that are crowded together in a tight or cramped space. The first recorded use of the phrase in print is from the year 1908, in a book called *The Cruise of the Dry Dock* by T. W. H. Crosland.

252. Best of both worlds

The origin of the phrase "the best of both worlds" is unclear, but it has been part of the English language since the late 1800s. The earliest known usage of the expression can be traced back to the novel *Westward Ho!* by the English writer and clergyman Charles Kingsley, published in 1855. However, it is believed that the term existed even before that. The idiom has religious undertones that refer to the two worlds of life and afterlife. In this context, it suggests that a person who leads a virtuous life, and does good deeds for others, will be able to enjoy the fruits of their labor both in this life and in the next. Another theory is that the idiom originated from philosophy, where the idea of having the best of both worlds is achieved by balancing different opposing ideas or beliefs. The phrase became popular in the mid and late 1900s. Despite the uncertainty of its origin, it is commonly understood to mean having the best of two different options without having to choose between them.

253. Lose your marbles

To "lose your marbles" refers to a situation in which someone becomes confused, irrational, or mentally unstable. It originated in the mid-20th century and is derived from the idea of losing actual marbles, which were small glass or ceramic balls that could roll off and become lost. The phrase is a common idiom in English and is often used to convey a sense of disorientation. It could be put mildly in conversation, as a self-deprecating comment about oneself or in a more severe context of mental illness.

254. Eager beaver

An "eager beaver" describes a person who is enthusiastic, hardworking, and eager to get things done. The phrase is thought to have originated in the United States in the early 20th century, specifically during World War I, where it was used to describe the very eager recruits who were willing to do anything to impress their commanding officers. The origin of the phrase comes from the idea of a beaver, which is a hardworking and industrious animal. Beavers are large rodents that are well known for their skill of building dams that are very large compared to their size. It's important to note that this term is commonly used in a positive way to refer to someone who is hardworking and enthusiastic, but it can also be used in a negative way to describe someone who is overly eager and can be perceived as pushy or impatient.

255. This ain't my first rodeo

"This ain't my first rodeo" is a colloquial phrase that is used to express the speaker's experience and competence in a particular situation. The term means that the speaker is not a novice and has dealt with similar situations before, and is not easily surprised or flustered. The idiom is frequently used to assert one's superiority when a less experienced person is trying to give advice to the more experienced person. The word "ain't" is a slang contraction for "it is not" and the word "rodeo" refers to a contest where cowboys and cowgirls exhibit their skills in various events such as bull riding, bronco riding, and calf roping. The idiom "this ain't my first rodeo" is generally traced back to the movie *Mommie Dearest*.

256. Fifth wheel

The term "fifth wheel" has its origins in the early days of horse-drawn vehicles, specifically wagons and carriages. These vehicles often had four wheels and a central hub on which the fifth wheel was mounted. This fifth wheel served as a support for the vehicle, allowing it to turn more smoothly and easily. However, when a fifth wheel was not needed, it was considered to be an unnecessary addition and a hindrance. The phrase is now used to describe someone or something that is not needed or unnecessary in a situation, often referring to a person who is not part of a group or project and is considered to be an outsider. The term was first recorded in the early 1800s.

257. Cut corners

To "cut corners" refers to taking shortcuts or doing things in a less thorough or efficient manner in order to save money or time and is used to convey a sense of laziness or a lack of attention to detail. It is believed to have originated in the 19th century and likely developed from the literal practice of cutting corners when taking a shortcut or making a journey. In this context, the phrase refers to the idea of taking a shorter or more direct route, often at the expense of efficiency or thoroughness. Now, the expression is used more broadly to describe any situation in which someone takes shortcuts to save time or money.

258. Bear a grudge

To "bear a grudge" means that someone continues to harbor resentment or anger towards someone else, often over a perceived slight that was done to them. It originated from old English in the 16th century and is derived from the idea of bearing or carrying a burden, in this case a negative feeling or emotion. Today, the phrase is mostly used to convey a sense of bitterness or resentment.

259. Chasing rainbows

"Chasing rainbows" refers to the pursuit of something that is unattainable or unlikely to be achieved. It is often used to describe the pursuit of dreams or goals that are unrealistic to attain or to suggest that someone is wasting their time or energy on something that will not bring them any tangible results. The origin of this phrase is likely derived from the phenomenon of a rainbow, which is an optical illusion caused by the refraction of light through water droplets. Rainbows are often seen as symbols of hope and promise, but they are also transient and elusive, and it is impossible to reach or touch one. The idea of chasing something that is fleeting and unattainable is what gives this expression its meaning.

260. Down for the count

The idiom "down for the count" refers to a situation in which someone is unable to continue with a particular activity or task, often due to injury, illness, or exhaustion. It originated in the early 20th century and is derived from the sport of boxing, in which a fighter is considered to be "down for the count" if they are knocked down to the ground and unable to get up within a certain amount of time (usually as long as it takes the referee to count to ten). In modern time, the phrase is used to convey a sense of defeat or incapacity.

Did You Know?

The tongue is the only muscle in the human body that is attached at only one end. This makes it unique among all the other muscles in the body, which are attached at both ends and work in pairs to produce movement. The tongue is responsible for various functions, including speaking, swallowing, and tasting. It is also a very strong and flexible muscle that can move in various directions to help us eat and form words.

There are more possible iterations of a game of chess than there are atoms in the observable universe. Chess is a complex game with a large number of possible moves and outcomes, making it difficult to calculate the exact number of iterations. However, it is estimated that there are over 10^{120} possible combinations of moves in a game of chess. This is an astronomical number and far larger than the estimated number of atoms in the observable universe, which is estimated to be around 10^{80}.

The Great Pyramid of Giza, one of the Seven Wonders of the World, is estimated to weigh around six million tons. It was built over 4,500 years ago and is one of the most impressive structures ever created by humans. It is made up of over two million blocks of granite and limestone, each weighing an average of two and a half tons. The sheer size and weight of the pyramid is amazing and it is a testament to the engineering and architectural skills of the ancient Egyptians.

261. Hop, skip, and jump

The phrase "hop, skip, and a jump" has its roots in the world of dance, first appearing in the early 1700s as "hop, step, and jump." It referred to a specific sequence of movements in a dance routine. However, by the mid 1700s, the term had evolved to "hop, skip, and a jump," while still referring to a dance move. It wasn't until the early to mid 1800s that the expression began to take on its current meaning of describing a short distance. The idea is that if a destination is just a "hop, skip, and jump" away then it is close by and wouldn't take long to travel to.

262. In hot water

The idiomatic expression "in hot water" refers to a state of trouble or adversity. This phrase has roots that can be traced back to the 17th century and is evocative of being immersed in water that is of such a high temperature as to cause burning. The act of pouring boiling water on intruders or foes was a widespread practice in ancient times, serving as a form of defense or punishment. This was executed from an elevated position, such as an upper-floor window or castle rampart, and was intended to force the unwanted visitors to retreat. The experience of being doused with boiling water would have been a harrowing one.

263. Rose-colored glasses

The expression "rose-colored glasses" refers to a tendency to view things in an overly positive or optimistic light. The phrase has been in use since 1861, as recorded in *Tom Brown at Oxford* where it is described as an attitude of cheerful optimism of seeing everything in an attractive, pleasant light. Although the term is often used to describe someone who is unwilling to see the negative aspects of a situation or person, it is also acknowledged that everyone wears these "spectacles" of optimism occasionally. The renowned French singer and songwriter Edith Piaf wrote and sang a song called "La vie en rose," which is the French equivalent of the phrase "rose-colored glasses," and further emphasizes the connection between the idiom and the idea of seeing the world through a positive and optimistic lens.

264. On the ball

"On the ball" is a colloquial expression that suggests a person is alert, ready, and well-informed. The phrase is frequently used to indicate that someone is paying close attention to the current situation and is able to respond quickly and effectively. It can also convey the idea that a person is well-organized and able to manage multiple tasks simultaneously. The term has its origins in sports, specifically in games that involve a ball. The idiom is derived from the earlier expression "keep your eye on the ball," which is a piece of advice that has been given to players of various ball games such as cricket, golf, croquet, and baseball. The phrase is found in early records of these sports and many people believe that baseball is the source of this idiomatic expression.

265. Yada yada

"Yada yada" is a colloquial term that denotes the act of succinctly summarizing or skipping over a lengthy or insignificant conversation or action. The phrase is believed to have originated in vaudeville (a theatrical genre of entertainment born in France at the end of the 19th century), with the spelling "yaddeyahdah" being used by Lenny Bruce, an American comedian active in the 1960s. The resurgence of popularity of the expression can be attributed to the "Seinfeld" television series, and it is often rendered with three "yadas" rather than two. People usually use "yada yada" in casual conversation as a way of skipping over unimportant or uninteresting details.

266. On cloud nine

The expression "on cloud nine" refers to a state of extreme happiness. It originated from the phrase "in cloud-cuckoo-land," which was used to describe a state of being out of touch with reality or disconnected from the world. The term "on cloud nine" is now used to describe a state of contentment and often conveys a sense of being in a dream-like state or being disconnected from the everyday world. It's applicable in a wide range of situations, including happiness in romantic relationships, career successes, and other events or experiences that bring great joy or fulfillment.

267. Spin doctor

The term "spin doctor" is used to describe a person who is skilled at manipulating or shaping public opinion or perception, often in a way that is misleading or deceptive. It originated in the United Kingdom in the 1980s and it comes from the idea of spinning, or twisting, the truth or facts in order to present a particular point of view or interpretation. It is often employed in a negative or critical way, implying that the person is engaging in unethical or dishonest behavior; however, it can also be used more generally to describe any person who is skilled at manipulating or changing public opinion, regardless of their intentions or motivations.

268. Foaming at the mouth

The phrase "foaming at the mouth" is used to describe a person who is extremely angry or agitated. Its origins can be traced back to the medical condition known as rabies. Rabies is a viral disease that affects the nervous system of warm-blooded animals, including humans. One of the most common symptoms of rabies is excessive salivation, which leads to the production of foam or froth around the animal's mouth. This symptom has been observed since ancient times, as described in the texts of Hippocrates and Galen. The appearance of animals affected with rabies, in which they literally foam at the mouth while in a blind stupor that can include attacks that look like they stem from anger or rage, is the origin of the term.

269. A left handed compliment

The idiom "a left-handed compliment" refers to a remark or compliment that is meant to be complimentary but is actually insincere, derogatory, or has a sarcastic meaning. The origin is thought to be related to the idea of a left-handed compliment being "backhanded." The earliest written use of this phrase dates back to the late 19th century. It appears in a book called *The Man with Two Left Feet* by P.G. Wodehouse, which was published in 1917. The book includes the line, "It was one of those left-handed compliments that are more offensive than open abuse."

270. Fool's errand

The term "fool's errand" means a useless or pointless pursuit. It often describes something that is a waste of time or effort, and is unlikely to achieve any worthwhile result. The origin of this idiom is thought to be related to the idea of a fool or someone who is not very intelligent or capable. The earliest written use of this phrase dates back to the 16th century. It appears in a book called *The Proverbs, Epigrams, and Miscellanies* by John Heywood, which was published in 1562. The book includes the line, "Send not a boy on a man's errand, nor a fool on any errand."

Did You Know?

Vatican City, officially called the Holy See, is a tiny city-state located in the heart of Rome, Italy. It is the smallest independent state in the world by both area and population. It is the headquarters of the Roman Catholic Church and the residence of the Pope, making it a major center of pilgrimage for millions of Catholics worldwide.

The human lung has a surface area of about 753 square feet (seventy square meters), which is roughly equivalent to the size of a tennis court. This large surface area allows for efficient gas exchange between the lungs and the bloodstream, which is crucial for breathing and getting oxygen to the body's cells. The lungs are also responsible for removing waste gases like carbon dioxide from the bloodstream, ensuring that the body's internal environment remains healthy.

The human body can survive without food for approximately one month, but without water, survival is limited to only one week or less. Water is an essential component in maintaining balance in the body's various functions and performing crucial processes, such as digestion, transportation of nutrients, regulation of body temperature, and elimination of waste. The human body consists of 50-75% water and even small decreases in hydration levels can result in serious consequences such as fatigue, headaches, dry mouth, dizziness, and in severe cases, unconsciousness or death. The time an individual can survive without water varies based on factors such as age, health, climate, and physical activity levels, with an average of three to five days for an adult. It is important to consume sufficient amounts of water daily, with a recommended intake of eight glasses or half a gallon (two liters), although individual needs may vary.

271. On his last legs

The idiom "on his last legs" means to be near the end or close to failing or collapsing. It suggests that the person or thing in question is in a weakened state and may not be able to continue for much longer. There are a few possible origins for this phrase, including the idea of a person or animal being near the end of their physical or mental endurance and being unable to walk on their legs any longer, or the idea of a person or thing being in a weakened state, and being at risk of failing or collapsing. It is often used to suggest that the person or thing in question is in a precarious state and that it may not be able to continue for much longer.

272. Shotgun wedding

A "shotgun wedding" refers to a wedding that takes place under pressure or coercion, often due to an unplanned pregnancy. It often encompasses a situation where one or both parties are forced into marriage due to societal or familial expectations. The origin of the phrase can be traced back to the 19th century in the United States, from the practice of using a shotgun to intimidate the man into marrying the woman with whom he had gotten pregnant.

273. In the fast lane

The phrase "in the fast lane" refers to a situation in which a person is moving or working at a fast pace, usually in a way that is intense or highly focused. It can also refer to a lifestyle or mindset that is characterized by fast-paced activity and a desire for success or achievement. The expression is often used to describe someone who is ambitious and driven, and who is always looking for new challenges or opportunities. The term is frequently employed in a positive way to praise someone's hard work and determination, but it can also be used in a negative way to suggest that someone is overburdened or overwhelmed by their busy schedule. The idiom emerged in the mid-20th century and was influenced by the metaphor of a highway or roadway with different lanes for different speeds. In this context, the "fast lane" would be the lane on the highway that is reserved for the fastest-moving traffic. The phrase may also have been influenced by the idea of "fast living," or a lifestyle that is characterized by fast-paced activity and a desire for success or achievement.

274. Fortune favors the bold

"Fortune favors the bold" is an idiomatic expression that means that people who take risks and are bold are more likely to be successful than those who are timid and hesitant. The origin of this expression can be traced back to ancient literature, specifically to the play titled *Phormio* by Roman playwright Terence in 161 BC, where the proverbial phrase "Fortis fortuna adiuvat" was used in Act 1, which means "fortune helps the brave." However, it's not the literal English translation of what Terence wrote. Later, the Roman poet Virgil used the phrase better in his epic poem *Aeneid*, saying "audentes Fortuna iuvat" which translates to "Fortune favors the bold," where "Fortuna" is the name of the goddess of luck. There are several other versions of the term such as "fortune favors the brave," "fate favors the bold," "God favors the bold," "those who are willing to take a risk are often highly rewarded," and "bravery is oftentimes rewarded."

275. Looking to your laurels

The idiom "looking to your laurels" refers to a situation where steps are being taken to maintain or improve one's position or reputation, especially in relation to others who are competing or striving for similar goals. It originated in the 19th century and is derived from the ancient Greek tradition of awarding laurel wreaths to victors and other accomplished individuals as a symbol of honor and achievement. Nowadays, the phrase is mainly used to convey a sense of ambition or determination.

276. You can't judge a book by its cover

"You can't judge a book by its cover" is a way of saying that one should not look at the superficial characteristics of a person or object and make over-arching judgments. The origin of this phrase is from a 1944 edition of the journal *American Speech*, where it first appeared in the form "You can't judge a book by its binding." The phrase was popularized even more when it appeared in the 1946 murder mystery *Murder in the Glass Room* by Edwin Rolfe and Lester Fuller.

277. Big fish in a small pond

The phrase "big fish in a small pond" is frequently used to describe someone who has achieved a high level of status or accomplishment within a specific community or environment, but who may not have the same level of success or recognition in a larger, more competitive setting. The expression originated in the early 20th century and was used in the context of business or politics. It's inspired by the idea that a large fish will dominate a small body of water, but may struggle to compete in a bigger, tougher environment. In modern usage, the idiom is often employed to acknowledge or praise someone for their accomplishments within a specific context, while also suggesting that they may face challenges or setbacks if they try to expand their influence or success to a wider audience.

278. Pipe down

"Pipe down" is an expression that is used to tell someone to be quiet or stop talking. It originated in the 19th century in the context of ships at sea. In naval ships, pipes or whistles were used to signal different orders to the crew. When the order to "pipe down" was given, it meant that the crew should stop making noise and be quiet. Similarly, "pipe up" is an idiom that is used to tell someone to speak up or to speak louder. It originated from naval ships as well and when the order to "pipe up" was given, it meant that the crew should speak up and be heard. The context and the tone of the speaker are important to determine the correct meaning of the phrase.

279. Ins and outs

Geoffrey Chaucer, an English poet, first used the phrase "ins and outs" in his poem *Troilus and Criseyde* in the late 1300s. The term was used again within the political sphere in 1814 in the writings of Thomas Jefferson to describe two opposing political parties; the party in power was "in," and the opposing party was "out." Only in the 19th century did the idiom begin being used in the way we know it now. Nowadays, the phrase has a broader application, referring to the details or specifics of something, particularly its intricate or complex aspects. It is often used to express a thorough or complete understanding of something, including the small details or nuances.

280. To move at a snail's pace

"To move at a snail's pace" means to move very slowly or to progress very little. The phrase is commonly utilized to describe a situation that is taking a long time to develop or to describe someone who is working at a very slow speed. The expression is a metaphor, comparing the movement of a person or thing to that of a snail, which is known for its slow pace of movement. The origin of the idiom can be traced back to Shakespeare's play, *Richard III*, spoken by King Richard in act 4, scene 3, where he says, "Delay leads impotent and snail-paced beggary."

Did You Know?

A cockroach can live for several weeks without its head due to their ability to breathe through tiny holes in their bodies, rather than their mouths. Cockroaches have a decentralized nervous system, which means that their vital functions are controlled by individual ganglia, or clusters of nerve cells, rather than by a single brain. As a result, a cockroach can continue to move, feed, and even mate for a few weeks after losing its head, until it ultimately succumbs to dehydration.

Sloths are known for their slow-moving and unique lifestyle, and only defecate once a week. They are arboreal mammals that spend the majority of their lives hanging upside down in trees. Sloths have a low metabolism and move slowly to conserve energy, which also makes them excellent at avoiding predators.

An octopus has three hearts, which are essential for pumping blood throughout its eight limbs and complex nervous system. Octopuses are also known for their ability to change color and texture to blend in with their surroundings, making them excellent at camouflage. This helps them evade predators or ambush prey, and they can rapidly change their appearance to match the colors and patterns of their surroundings.

Bats are known for their long lifespan relative to their size, with some species living over twenty years. They are the only mammals that can fly and have unique adaptations that allow them to live for such a long time, including a slow metabolism, low reproductive rate, and the ability to enter into a state of torpor, or reduced activity, during winter months to conserve energy. Bats play an important role in the ecosystem, as many species are pollinators or consume large quantities of insects, making them important for controlling pest populations.

281. Go cold turkey

The idiom "go cold turkey" means to stop using something suddenly and completely, especially a habit or addiction. It is often used in the context of quitting a habit such as smoking or drug use, and often implies the physical symptoms of withdrawal that may occur when someone stops using a substance abruptly. The origins of this expression are not entirely clear, but it is thought to have originated in the United States in the mid-20th century. One theory is that it refers to the goosebumps and "cold" skin that can occur during withdrawal from some substances, while another theory suggests that it may be a reference to the phrase "cold feet," which is used to describe someone who is having second thoughts or is reluctant to do something.

282. Burn one's boats

The idiomatic expressions "burn one's bridges" and "burn one's boats" have their origins in both ancient Roman military tactics as well as the story of the Spanish conquistador Hernán Cortés. The Roman armies would destroy bridges in order to stop the enemy from fleeing and to cut off their supply lines. They would also destroy their boats upon landing on the enemy's shore to eliminate the possibility of retreat, thus forcing them to fight to the death or victory. Similarly, when Cortés landed in Mexico in 1519, he ordered his men to burn their ships as a symbolic gesture to demonstrate to his men that they were now committed to the conquest of the Aztec Empire and that there was no turning back. Both of these historical events gave rise to the use of "burn one's bridges" or "burn one's boats," which are used to describe a situation where someone makes a bold and irreversible decision, such as quitting a job or ending a relationship, in which the individual commits to a course of action with no possibility of turning back.

283. Pony up

The term "pony up" means to pay or contribute money, usually in a specific or agreed upon amount. The expression is thought to have originated in the late 19th century and is believed to have come from the practice of using small coins called "ponies" in horse racing bets. However, there is also a theory that the term dates back to the 16th century and comes from the Latin phrase "legem pone" which is found in Psalm 119. This theory suggests that the term originated in Britain, and it was used on the Quarter Day, which is the first payday of the year (this day was March 25th). Although this theory is less common, it is still an explanation for the origin of the phrase "pony up."

284. Face the music

The idiom "face the music" means to accept the consequences of one's actions or to confront a difficult situation or unpleasant reality. It is commonly used to describe the act of taking responsibility and dealing with the consequences, even if they are difficult. The origin of this idiom is not entirely clear, but it might have come from the United States in the mid-19th century. One theory is that it may be a reference to the practice of holding a formal military court martial, where a soldier accused of an offense would be required to stand at attention and listen to the reading of the charges against them. Another theory is that it may be a reference to the practice of facing a firing squad, where a person accused of a crime would be required to stand and face the guns of their executioners. The earliest recorded use of the phrase "face the music" dates back to 1834, when it appeared in *The New Hampshire Statesman & State Journal*.

285. A hairsbreadth

The term "a hairsbreadth" describes an extremely narrow margin or distance. It originated in the United Kingdom in the 16th century and comes from the idea of a hair being thin and slender. The phrase suggests that the margin or distance in question is so small that it is almost imperceptible, similar to the width of a single hair. Today, the idiom is mainly used in a dramatic or suspenseful manner, implying that the margin or distance in question is so small that it could easily be missed or overlooked.

286. You look like a million dollars

"You look like a million dollars" is a compliment used to express that someone looks very attractive or impressive. The origin comes from the early 20th century when a million dollars was considered a large and impressive amount of money. To look like a million dollars was to look wealthy, successful, and put together. It originated in the United States, where the expression of wealth and success was particularly important in the 1920s, a period of great prosperity and social change. The phrase was commonly used in popular culture, such as in movies and songs, and it quickly became a commonly used expression of admiration. The expression has since evolved to be less focused on wealth and more on someone's overall appearance. Today it's used to express admiration for someone's physical appearance, as well as their style, grooming, and general sense of fashion.

287. Green fingers

The term "green fingers" is an expression describing someone who has a natural talent for gardening and cultivating plants. It is often used to portray a person who is skilled at growing flowers, fruits, and vegetables and who is able to make them thrive. The origins of the phrase are not entirely clear, but there are several possible sources. The first hypothesis suggests that it came from the discoloration of a gardener's hands from the exposure to algae and crushed leaves in the course of their work with plants. The second theory associates the term with the "Green Man," an archetypal symbol denoting the growth and vitality of plants in various ancient religious systems. The third theory suggests that it is modeled on the myth of the Midas touch, where a king's touch was said to transmute objects into gold. The expression "green thumb" is primarily the American version of the idiom, while "green fingers" is primarily the British version.

288. Don't give up your day job

"Don't give up your day job" is a sarcastic expression that is used to tell a person that they are not very good at something, especially when they haven't given a serious effort into the attempt. The phrase suggests that they should stick to their regular job, as they are not likely to succeed in the endeavor they are currently undertaking. The earliest recorded instance of this phrase is from a publication called *The Billboard* (Cincinnati, Ohio) on June 16th, 1951, in an article where it was quoted as, "Berle, I caught you on TV. Don't give up the day job."

289. The jury is out

The phrase "the jury is out" is commonly used in situations where there is ongoing debate, uncertainty, or lack of information about a particular issue. It can be applied in a variety of contexts, such as in politics, business, or science, to indicate that a decision or judgment has not yet been made and that more information is needed before a conclusion can be reached. The origin of the expression is traced back to the court system where juries hear cases and make decisions. The jury, made up of citizens, is responsible for listening to the evidence presented by both the prosecution and the defense, and then deliberate in secret to reach a verdict. The jury's decision, also known as the verdict, must be unanimous, meaning that all jurors must agree on the outcome. The jury deliberation is secret, hence the phrase "the jury is out" indicating that no one knows the outcome yet.

290. Game the system

The phrase "game the system" means to use clever tactics or strategies to gain an advantage within a particular system or process. The origins of this term can be traced back to the field of systems engineering in the mid-1970s, where it was used to describe the manipulation of systems to achieve a desired outcome. However, it did not become widely popular in general culture until the 1990s. The expression implies that the person using the tactics is aware of the rules and uses them to their advantage in a clever and cunning way. It is also frequently utilized in a negative way to describe someone who is perceived as manipulating or cheating to get ahead.

Did You Know?

The Amazon Rainforest, also known as the Amazon Jungle, is a vast and complex ecosystem that covers over 2.1 million square miles (5.4 square kilometers) and spans across nine countries in South America. It is home to an estimated 390 billion individual trees and thousands of species of plants and animals, many of which are not found anywhere else in the world. The Amazon is also known for its incredible biodiversity, with an estimated ten percent of the world's known species residing within its boundaries. The rainforest also plays a critical role in regulating the world's climate and weather patterns, as it helps to absorb carbon dioxide and release oxygen into the atmosphere.

The Galapagos Islands, located off the coast of Ecuador, are a unique and diverse ecosystem that have long been of interest to scientists and naturalists. The islands are home to a variety of species found nowhere else in the world, including giant tortoises, marine iguanas, and flightless cormorants. The Galapagos Islands were made famous by Charles Darwin, who visited them in 1835, and was inspired by the diversity of species he found there to develop his theory of evolution. The Galapagos Islands are also known for their stunning natural beauty, with crystal-clear waters, rugged volcanic landscapes, and abundant wildlife.

The Northern Lights (Aurora Borealis), are a natural light display that can be seen in the night sky in the northern hemisphere. They are caused by charged particles colliding with the Earth's atmosphere, which produces a beautiful and colorful display of light. The Northern Lights can be seen in various colors, including green, red, yellow, and blue, and are best viewed from dark and clear locations away from city lights.

291. Hand Over Fist

The origins of the idiom "hand over fist" are unclear, but it may have come about in the mid-19th century. One theory is that the phrase comes from how sailors used to haul in a ship's anchor by pulling on a rope with both hands, making a fist around the rope, and then quickly repeating the motion as they pulled it in. This action would have looked as if the sailors were grabbing the anchor with both hands and collecting it quickly, or "hand over fist." Another theory is that it comes from a person counting their money quickly and efficiently as if they were grabbing it with both hands and counting it rapidly. Regardless of its origins, the idiom is now used to describe someone quickly earning or acquiring something and in large amounts. It suggests that the person is receiving money or other resources at a swift pace, as if they are grabbing them with both hands.

292. Call it a day

The idiom "call it a day" means to stop working or to end a task for the day. The expression began with the phrase "call it half a day," which was originally recorded in 1838. This term was used to refer to employees who went home before the end of the workday and their attendance records would reflect that they had worked a half day. Later, the phrase was transformed into "call it a day," which means that work on that particular day is completely over. The first recorded use of this expression was in 1919.

293. Oddball

The term "oddball" can be used as a noun to refer to a person who is strange or unusual in some way, or as an adjective to describe something that is unusual or peculiar. One origin theory comes from the idea of a ball that is not perfectly round or symmetrical, and that may be considered unusual or dysfunctional. Another theory is that it may have been derived from the phrase "odd ball," with the word "ball" being used in the sense of "person." In any case, the word "oddball" has been in use in English since at least the 1950s, and it has become a widely used term to describe someone or something that is strange or peculiar.

294. Six of one, half a dozen of other

The idiom "six of one, half a dozen of the other" is used to indicate that two options or alternatives are roughly equal or interchangeable. The earliest known written use of the phrase can be found in the journal of Ralph Clark, a British naval officer, who wrote in 1790 while on a ship in the Pacific Ocean: "Of all the places in the World this is the greatest nest for Rascals it is impossible to trust any one of our men, hardly much more any of the Convicts, in Short there is no difference between Soldier Sailor or Convicts, there Six of the one and half a Dozen of the other." This entry illustrates how the phrase was originally used to describe the equivalence of two different groups of people, but over time, it has become a way to outline the equivalence of any two options.

295. At a crossroads

The term "at a crossroads" describes a situation where a person must make a decision that will have a significant impact on their future. The origin of this phrase comes from physical crossroads, where two or more roads intersect. Historically, crossroads were considered important decision-making points as they offered the opportunity to choose a different direction to travel. A number of ancient tribes utilized crossroads as sites for religious offerings, while during the Christian era, individuals who were executed for crimes and those who perished by their own hand were frequently buried at crossroads. The notion of a symbolic crossroads, a pivotal moment where one must choose the direction to take, has a long history. Erasmus cites a piece from the Elegies of Theognis, a Greek poet from around 600 BC. The quote reads: "I stand at the crossroads" in its English translation.

296. Hail Mary

The phrase "Hail Mary" originated in American football and refers to a last-ditch effort, a desperate or improbable strategy made in the final seconds of a game. Its origins come from the Catholic prayer "Hail Mary" which is a traditional Catholic prayer asking for the intercession of the Virgin Mary, mother of Jesus, when one is in a difficult situation. The idea in American football is that the team member making the play does so while saying a prayer that it will be successful, and is typically when the quarterback throws a long pass into the end-zone in the final seconds before time runs out. The term can be traced back to the 1920s, when it was used by the Four Horsemen of Notre Dame, an outstanding group of players on the college team, to describe a desperate, last-minute forward pass. However, it gained wider use in 1975, when Dallas Cowboys quarterback Roger Staubach made a successful fifty yard pass, later referred to as a Hail Mary pass, during a game. When asked about it later, Staubach said, "I just closed my eyes and said a Hail Mary." This play and the comment brought the term into mainstream use.

297. Hot to trot

The idiom "hot to trot" has its origins in the world of horse racing and horseback riding. The phrase refers to a horse that is ready and eager to run, and was first used in the early 1900s to describe a horse that was yearning to start a race or begin a ride. The expression was later adopted to refer to people who are eager or excited to do something, and is commonly used to portray a person who is enthusiastic or ready to begin a task or activity.

298. Cold-hearted

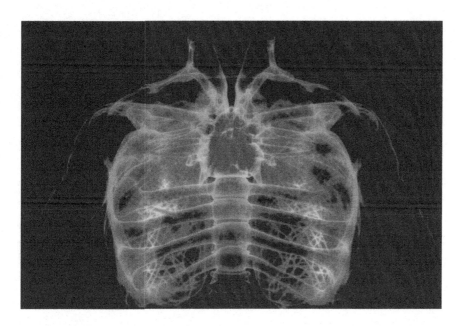

The phrase "cold-hearted" is used to describe a person who is emotionally detached, unsympathetic, or lacking in compassion or empathy. The origin of this idiom comes from the metaphor of comparing a person's emotions to the temperature of the heart. For centuries, people have believed that the heart is the seat of emotions and that a cold-hearted person is one who lacks warmth and compassion in their emotional life. It's important to note that some people might be perceived as cold-hearted due to certain emotional or psychological disorders and not by choice, so this phrase should be used with caution.

The origin of the idiomatic phrase "clear as mud" comes to us from the late 19th century. The idiom is an example of an oxymoron, a figure of speech in which two opposing or contradictory terms are combined. In this case, the word "clear" is used to describe something that is easy to understand, while "mud" is used to represent something that is murky and difficult to see through. The phrase is thought to have originated as a way to express frustration or confusion about something that is supposed to be explained or understood, but is instead difficult to grasp.

300. The devil is in the details

"The devil is in the details" is used to express that small, seemingly insignificant details can cause big problems or difficulties. The phrase originated in the late 19th century, with the earliest citation recorded in the late 1880s. It was first used by Friedrich Wilhelm Nietzsche, a German philosopher and poet, who is quoted as saying "Der Teufel steckt im Detail," which translates to "The devil is in the details." Nietzsche's use of the expression may have been a play on the original phrase "God is in the details," which means that a higher power has a hand in the success and truthfulness of a completed work. Nowadays, when we say "the devil is in the details," it has a similar connotation to "read the fine print" or "pay attention" in that it is a warning to be on the lookout for the small, often forgotten things.

Did You Know?

There are more stars in the observable universe than there are grains of sand on all the beaches on Earth. The observable universe is estimated to contain around two trillion galaxies, each of which contains billions of stars. The exact number of stars in the universe is not known, but it is estimated to be in the hundreds of billions of billions, making it impossible to count the number of stars in the observable universe. The estimated number of grains of sand on all the beaches on Earth, on the other hand, is estimated to be around 7.5×10^{18}.

One light-year is the distance that light travels in one year. Light travels at a speed of 299,792,458 meters per second (in a vacuum), making it the fastest thing in the universe. A light-year is the distance that light travels in one year, which is approximately 5.88 trillion miles (9.46 trillion kilometers).

The Sun is one of over a hundred billion stars in the Milky Way galaxy. The Milky Way is a barred spiral galaxy that is part of the Local Group of galaxies, which also includes the Andromeda Galaxy, the Triangulum Galaxy, and about fifty-four other smaller galaxies. The Sun is located in one of the spiral arms of the Milky Way and it is estimated that there are at least 100 billion stars in our galaxy alone, with possibly even more undiscovered.

A black hole is formed when a massive star collapses under the force of its own gravity. The gravitational pull of a black hole is so strong that it does not allow anything, not even light, to escape once it has crossed the event horizon. The event horizon is the point of no return, beyond which anything that enters is pulled into the black hole, never to escape again. Black holes are some of the most mysterious and fascinating objects in the universe, and scientists are still learning about their properties and behaviors.

301. Take to the cleaners

The idiom "to take to the cleaners" means to cheat or defraud someone out of a large amount of money or resources. It is frequently used in the context of gambling or legal disputes, where one person threatens to beat the other in a gamble or to sue them in court. The phrase is thought to have evolved from an older idiom, "to clean someone out," which means to strip someone of their money. It is believed to have come into use in the 1920s, around the time when dry cleaning establishments began to crop up. The metaphor of cleaning or laundering money is often used to refer to situations where someone is taken advantage of or duped in a way that leaves them financially or materially worse off. The earliest written use of this expression appears in *The New Dictionary of American Slang* by Harold Wentworth and Stuart Berg Flexner, which was published in 1960.

302. If worse comes to worst

When someone says "if worse comes to worst," it means that they are preparing for the least desirable outcome, almost with resignation that it will come true. This idiom dates back to 1596, in a pamphlet written by Thomas Dash in which he compared dying by drowning versus dying by burning. He wrote, "If the worst comes to the worst, a good swimmer may do much." The phrase has since been used by the likes of Charles Dickens and Charlotte Brontë. Initially, the idiom presented the idea of a worst-case hypothetical scenario that becomes a reality. In 1719, Daniel Defoe wrote *Robinson Crusoe* and used a slightly altered version of the expression when the titular character said, "If the worse came to the worst, I could but die." The term gained a more negative connotation, as it hints that the situation is already negative and has the possibility of becoming more so.

303. Graveyard shift

The phrase "graveyard shift" refers to a work schedule that takes place during the overnight hours, typically from midnight to 8 a.m. The idea of a shift in the middle of the night being like a graveyard is likely a metaphor, as night is when everyone else (working a normal shift) is sleeping, the streets are deserted, and the world is as quiet as a graveyard. The expression "graveyard shift" originated in the US in the late 1800s, as mine and factory owners discovered they could increase production by operating twenty-four hours a day. The term conveys a less-than-favorable schedule and hints at the worker missing out on a typical social life.

304. Kill two birds with one stone

Sources believe that this phrase originated from the Greek mythology story of Daedalus and Icarus, where Daedalus killed two birds with one stone to get their feathers in order to make wings. The expression first appeared in writing in 1656, in *The Questions Concerning Liberty, Necessity, and Chance by Thomas Hobbes*, where he wrote, "T.H. thinks to kill two birds with one stone, and satisfies two arguments with one answer, whereas in truth he satisfieth neither." Today, the idiom is used more broadly to mean to accomplish two things simultaneously or in a single effort, often in an efficient or cost-effective manner. It is often used to suggest that it is possible to achieve multiple goals or objectives with a single action or effort rather than having to devote separate resources or time to each task.

305. Draw a blank

The expression "draw a blank" is a colloquial way of describing when someone is unable to remember or recall something, or when someone is not able to find the information they are looking for. The origins of this phrase can be traced back to the late 19th century and Tudor, England, where the first national lottery was established by Queen Elizabeth in 1567. The operation of the lottery involved the insertion of slips of paper, each bearing the name of a participant, into one container, while an equivalent quantity of slips, some denoting rewards and others being blank, were placed in another receptacle. A simultaneous drawing of pairs of tickets from both containers would result in a pairing between a participant and a prize. However, it was not uncommon for the drawing to produce a blank slip, leading to the participant "drawing a blank" and winning no reward.

The expression "keeping up with the Joneses" refers to the act of trying to maintain the same level of material possessions or social status as one's neighbors or peers. It suggests a desire to fit in or be seen as successful or affluent and can often involve spending beyond one's means or engaging in conspicuous consumption to keep up with others. The expression was first used in the 1913 comic *Keeping Up With the Joneses*, created by Arthur R. Momand. The comic centers around the McGinnis family and their constant endeavor to keep up with their neighbors, the Joneses. The Joneses remained unseen throughout the comic strip, although they were regularly mentioned. As a generic last name, "Jones" has been widely used to identify neighbors and other rivals.

307. Palm off

The term "palm off" refers to a situation in which someone tries to deceive or trick someone else by selling them something of poor quality or by pretending that something is of higher value than it actually is. It is thought to have originated in the 19th century and is likely derived from the idea of "palming off" a fake or inferior object by quickly slipping it into someone's hand without their noticing. Today, the phrase is a common idiom in English and is commonly used to convey a sense of deception or trickery.

308. Frog in one's throat

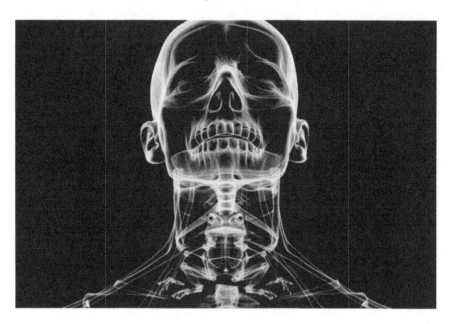

The idiom "frog in one's throat" is used to describe the sensation of having a lump in one's throat or difficulty swallowing or speaking. It originated in the United Kingdom in the 19th century and comes from the idea of a frog being a small, slimy animal that might be difficult to swallow. The phrase suggests that the person in question is experiencing a similar sensation of having something stuck in their throat that is causing difficulty swallowing or speaking. It is often used in a casual or lighthearted manner, implying that the person is experiencing a temporary or minor issue with their throat. However, it can also be used more seriously to describe a more persistent or severe issue with the throat.

309. Get hitched

"Get hitched" is an idiomatic expression that means to get married. The origin of this phrase is unique to America and can be traced back to the mid-1800s. The expression compares getting married to teaming a pair of horses to pull a wagon or farm implement. It implies that the couple is now connected to each other and will work together to pull their life together. The phrase is a metaphor for the act of getting married and it is not meant to be an insult to the people in question; the expression is a testament to their compatibility. The practice of "hitching" a horse or other animal to a wagon or other vehicle in order to pull it was a common practice among farmers who only hitched teams of horses who had matched temperaments or whose temperaments complemented each other's.

310. Monkey business

The expression "monkey business" is rooted in the term "monkeyshine," which originated in 1832 and referred to a dishonorable act. In England, parents warned their children against bad conduct referred to as "monkey tricks." The idiom "monkey business" was first recorded in print in 1883 in W. Peck's Bad Boy, where it was used to warn against any sneaky or underhanded behavior. The phrase implies that the person or people involved are behaving in a way that is mischievous or dishonest and it has been used to describe illegal or unethical activities too.

Did You Know?

- The word "algorithm" comes from the name of the mathematician Al-Khwarizmi, who was a 9th-century Persian scholar. Al-Khwarizmi wrote a book called *Kitab al-Jabr wa-l-Muqabilah*, which means "The Book of Restoration and Balance," which contained a set of rules for solving mathematical problems.
- The word "tycoon" comes from the Japanese "taikun," which means "great lord." It was originally used to refer to the shogun, the military ruler of Japan, but it later came to be used as a term for a wealthy and powerful business person.
- The word "cocktail" comes from the French "coquetier," which means "egg cup." The term originally described a drink that was served in an egg-shaped glass.
- The word "chaos" comes from the Greek "khaos," which means "vast chasm or void." In Greek mythology, Chaos was the personification of the void or the emptiness that existed before the creation of the universe.

311. Lo and behold

The idiom "lo and behold" is an expression of surprise and emphasis, and it is often used to introduce something unexpected or remarkable. The phrase is thought to have originated from Middle English, specifically from the phrase "lo, behold!" which was used to express surprise or emphasis. The phrase became popular in the 16th century and has been used widely in literature and everyday speech since then. Both "lo" and "behold" are derived from Old English, with "lo" meaning "look" and "behold" meaning "give regard to" and "belong to." The phrase can be found in the King James Bible in 1611, where it says "And Abraham said; Behold, to mee thou has given no seed: and loe, one borne in my house is mine heire."

312. No pain, no gain

The expression "no pain, no gain" suggests that one must endure discomfort and exert effort in order to achieve a desired outcome, often in reference to building muscle or losing weight. It originated in the 1980s as a catchphrase used by fitness gurus and personal trainers, and is often used to motivate people to continue working hard, even when feeling tired or discouraged. The concept of this phrase can also be found in ancient Greek literature, specifically in the play *Electra* by Sophocles written in the 5th century BC, where it is stated that "Nothing truly succeeds without pain, nothing succeeds without toil, there is no success without hard work." This reinforces the idea that one can't expect to achieve something without putting in the effort.

313. All bark and no bite

The idiom "all bark and no bite" vividly captures the idea of someone who talks tough or boasts confidently, but ultimately fails to follow through with meaningful action. It likens the situation to a dog that barks aggressively but doesn't actually attack. This expression dates back to the 19th century and is believed to have origins in the behavior of animals. Although no specific written record of its earliest use exists, the idiom's metaphorical essence has remained remarkably consistent over time. In contemporary usage, "all bark and no bite" is playfully employed to humorously criticize individuals or situations where grandiose claims or threats lack genuine substance or force. It serves as a gentle reminder that actions speak louder than words, adding a touch of insight and whimsy to conversations about bravado and authenticity.

314. Know the ropes

To "know the ropes" means to be familiar with the ins and outs of a particular system, procedure, or activity. It suggests that the person has a high level of expertise or experience in a particular area and can navigate it with confidence and skill. This expression came about in the mid-16th to mid-19th centuries when sailing was the most common way of long-distance travel, and knowing how to sail was a highly valued skill. Before steamships were invented, many of a ship's operations were conducted via ropes and pulleys. To "know the ropes" meant that a person knew precisely which ropes had to be used for a specific function.

315. Runs the gamut/Run the gauntlet

The word "gamut" comes from the Latin language and means "the whole range" or "all the notes." It was first used in medieval music theory to describe the range of notes in a diatonic scale, from the lowest to the highest. As music theory evolved, the gamut was divided into smaller parts called hexachords, which were a series of six notes. By the 18th century, the term "gamut" came to be used more metaphorically, to describe a complete range of anything. In other words, if something "runs the gamut" it means it covers all aspects or all the variations of something. The idiom "to run the gauntlet" means to undergo a severe test or punishment, often involving physical abuse. The phrase is thought to have originated in the 17th century and it comes from a military punishment used in the past. In this punishment, a person was made to run between two lines of soldiers who would beat or strike the person as they ran through. This practice is known as "running the gauntlet" and the expression is used to describe any situation in which someone is subjected to severe punishment or harassment.

316. Zero-sum game

The phrase "zero-sum game" is an economic and game theory term used to describe a situation in which one person's gain is directly proportional to another person's loss. It is a situation where the total amount of resources is fixed and any gain by one person results in an equal loss by another person. The expression was first coined by John von Neumann and Oskar Morgenstern in their 1944 book *Theory of Games and Economic Behavior*. The concept of zero-sum game is often used to describe competitive situations such as business, sports, and politics.

317. Eat like a horse

The idiom "eat like a horse" refers to someone who eats a large quantity of food or eats very frequently. It originated in the 19th century and is derived from the observation that horses are known for their ability to eat huge amounts of food. Horses have a unique digestive system that allows them to eat large amounts of food at one time, and to extract the maximum amount of nutrition from it. They have a large stomach that can hold up to fifteen gallons (fifty-seven liters) of food, and they are able to graze for most of the day. In literature and popular culture, this phrase is often used in a humorous or exaggerating way, to convey that someone eats a lot of food, but not always in a negative way. It can also be used to describe someone who is eating in an indiscriminate way, without manners or delicacy.

318. Snake-oil salesman

The term "snake-oil salesman" describes someone who sells fraudulent or ineffective goods or services, with the implication that the salesperson is deceitful and untrustworthy. The expression is derived from the sale of "snake oil," a supposed cure-all that was often hawked by traveling salesmen in the 19th century. The origins of the phrase can be traced back to the early 19th century when Chinese immigrants in America working on the transcontinental railroad brought with them a traditional Chinese remedy for joint pain made from the oil of the Chinese water snake. Salesmen, who were not Chinese, began to sell their own versions of the remedy and often used the oil from other animals such as rattlesnakes, claiming it had the same medicinal properties. These salesmen were known to be dishonest, exaggerating the effectiveness of their products and often using dangerous or ineffective ingredients. As a result, the idiom "snake oil salesman" became synonymous with a con artist who sells fake or ineffective goods.

319. Blow off steam

To "blow off steam" means to release pent-up emotions or energy, often through physical or verbal expression. It is commonly used to describe the act of venting one's feelings or frustrations in order to reduce stress. There are two theories about the origins of this idiom. The first is that it is a reference to the way in which steam is released from a pressure valve in order to prevent an explosion or other catastrophic events. When a pressure valve is released, steam is allowed to escape in a controlled manner, preventing the build-up of pressure that could lead to an explosion. In a similar way, the idiom "blow off steam" may describe the act of releasing pent-up emotions or energy in a controlled manner in order to prevent a build-up of stress or tension. The second theory is that it may be a reference to the way in which steam locomotives release steam through their exhaust pipes in order to move forward. In this context, the idiom may have been used to describe the act of releasing energy or emotions in order to move forward or to relieve tension.

320. Take the mickey out of someone

To "take the mickey out of someone" means to tease or make fun of someone in a playful and good-natured way. It originated in the early 20th century in England, specifically in the Cockney dialect spoken in the East End of London. The word "mickey" is a slang term that was used to refer to a fool or an easy target for teasing. The phrase "taking the mickey" is believed to have come from the expression "taking the Mickey Bliss," which was a reference to a famous music hall song and stage act of the time. The act featured a man dressed as a woman named Mickey Bliss, who was often the butt of jokes and pranks.

Did You Know?

- The word "apocalypse" comes from the Greek "apokalypsis," which means "revelation." It is used to describe a catastrophic event or the end of the world.
- The word "petroleum" comes from the Latin "petra," which means "rock," and "oleum," which means "oil." It refers to a type of oil that is found in rock formations and is used as a fuel and a raw material for a variety of products.
- The word "kiwi" comes from the Maori word "kiwi," which is the name of a flightless bird native to New Zealand. The fruit was given this name because it is native to New Zealand and has a brown, fuzzy skin similar to the skin of the kiwi bird.
- The word "sherbet" comes from the Turkish "şerbet," which means "drink." It refers to a type of sweet, fruity drink that is made from fruit juice, water, and sugar.

321. Cheap as chips

The idiom "as cheap as chips" is a British phrase describing something that is inexpensive. The expression originated from the low cost of fish and chips, a traditional British meal that was popular among working-class people. Fish and chips were a cheap and readily available food item that could be purchased from street vendors or fish and chip shops. The phrase is typically used to indicate that something is very affordable, or that it offers good value for money.

322. Storm in a teacup

A "storm in a teacup" describes a situation that is being blown out of proportion or made to seem more significant or serious than it really is. It originated in the United Kingdom in the 17th century and comes from the idea of a teacup being a small and delicate container that is not capable of holding a large or intense storm. Nowadays, the expression is often used in a casual or lighthearted manner, implying that the situation is not particularly important or worth getting worked up over. Despite its lighthearted tone, the idiom can also be used to express frustration or annoyance with someone who is overreacting or making a big deal out of a minor issue.

323. Put something on ice

The expression "put something on ice" means to delay or postpone, usually temporarily, and can be used in a variety of contexts, such as business, politics, or personal matters. There are two different theories about the origins of this idiom. The first theory is that it comes from the idea of storing food in a cold place, such as a refrigerator or an icebox, in order to preserve it, suggesting that the idiom originally referred to the act of delaying the use or consumption of something by storing it in a cold place. The second theory is that the it is related to the expression "put something on hold," which means to delay or postpone something, suggesting that the idiom originally referred to the act of holding something in a state of inactivity.

324. The leopard never changes its spots

"The leopard never changes its spots" is a proverb that means that people do not change their basic nature or inherent character. The origins of this idiom can be traced back to ancient cultures, where the leopard was recognized as a powerful and majestic animal that was known for its distinctive spots. The saying reflects the belief that people cannot change the fundamental aspects of their personality, just as a leopard cannot change its spots. The phrase was first seen in the Old Testament and was used in Jeremiah 13:23, where the Hebrew prophet Jeremiah said: "Can the Ethiopian change his skin, or the leopard its spots?"

325. Blow smoke

"Blow smoke" is an idiom that means to make false or empty statements or promises, or to deceive or mislead someone. It originated from the act of smoking, as the phrase is often used to describe situations where someone is exhaling smoke from their mouth or nose. In modern usage, the expression describes situations where someone is trying to deceive or mislead others by making false or exaggerated claims, or by making promises that they do not intend to keep. It's commonly used as a way to suggest that someone is being dishonest and that their words should not be taken at face value.

326. Third time's the charm

The idiom "third time's the charm" is used to express the idea that the third attempt at something will be successful, often after two previous unsuccessful attempts. The origin of this phrase is likely ancient, as things that come in sets of three have often been associated with good luck due to their similarity with the Holy Trinity of Christianity. The earliest documented use of the expression in written form can be traced back to Elizabeth Barrett Browning's work, *Letters Addressed to R.H. Horne*, published in 1839, where it is noted that "The luck of the third adventure is proverbial," implying that the expression was already in widespread usage during that era. The saying is commonly employed in a jovial and hopeful manner, implying that persistence will lead to eventual triumph.

327. Hook line and sinker

To fall for something "hook, line, and sinker" means that someone has completely and uncritically accepted someone else's deception or lies. The phrase originated from the world of fishing, where a hook, line, and sinker are the basic components of a fishing rig. The hook is used to catch the fish, the line is used to reel it in, and the sinker is used to take the bait to the bottom of the water where the fish are located. The expression is thought to have come about in the late 1700s, and it is often used to indicate that someone has been completely taken in or deceived by something or someone, usually in a situation where they have been tricked or duped.

328. To pitch in

The idiom "to pitch in" is believed to have originated in the late 19th century and it refers to the act of contributing to a task or activity, usually voluntarily. It comes from the noun "pitch" which means a throw or a toss, and the preposition "in" indicating that one is participating or getting involved. The phrase originated in the mid-1800s from the practice of pitching hay or other materials onto a pile or into a barn. The term then started to be used more broadly to refer to any kind of voluntary participation or contribution to a task or activity.

329. It's not rocket science

The expression "it's not rocket science" is used to describe a task or concept that is not difficult or complicated. Rocket science is considered to be a complex and challenging field, and the phrase "it's not rocket science" is often used to contrast this complexity with something that is easier to understand or do. Most of the early citations of "not rocket science" relate to football, and the idiom has been used in this context to describe the simplicity of the game. A sports report in the Pennsylvania newspaper *The Daily Intelligencer*, from December 1985, stated: "Coaching football is not rocket science and it's not brain surgery. It's a game, nothing more."

330. In the loop and out of the loop

"In the loop" refers to being included in a group of people who are privy to important information or decision-making. The phrase originates from military terminology, where officers would communicate orders to soldiers in a feedback loop, keeping all personnel informed. If one is "in the loop," they are included in this group and have access to the specific knowledge shared among its members. On the other hand, being "out of the loop" means being excluded from this group and not having access to the information. The expression is based on the idea of a loop that goes around in a full circle, with those included in the loop being inside it, while those excluded are outside of it.

Did You Know?

- The word "majestic" comes from the Latin "majestas," which means "greatness" or "dignity." It describes something that is grand, stately, or impressive.
- The word "samurai" comes from the Japanese "saburau," which means "to serve." It was used to describe a member of a class of Japanese warriors who were trained in martial arts and were known for their bravery and loyalty.
- The word "bamboo" comes from the Kannada "bambu," which is the name of a type of grass that is native to India. It is a type of woody plant with hollow stems that are used for a variety of purposes, including building materials, food, and decorative items.
- The word "shampoo" comes from the Hindi "champoo," which means "to press." It refers to a product that is used to clean the hair and scalp.

331. Waste not, want not

The origins of the phrase "waste not, want not" are not entirely clear, with various writers, speakers, and everyday people having used it for centuries. It is believed to date back to at least 1772, and the first citation of it in the United States can be traced to 1932, when it appeared in the book *Topper Takes a Trip* by T. Smith. However, it is also suggested that the idiom may date back even further to the 1500s, with an alliterative version "Willful waste makes woeful want" also in use. Despite its vague beginning, the meaning of the phrase remains relevant today, serving as a reminder to use resources wisely and avoid unnecessary consumption.

332. Twist someone's arm

To "twist someone's arm" means to persuade or coax someone, especially when it is something they are reluctant to do. It usually refers to one person pressuring another person into getting what they want. The origins of this idiom are not clear, but it's likely that it has been in use for many centuries. The phrase "twist someone's arm" suggests the use of physical force, but it is generally used in a more metaphorical sense to describe the use of persuasive techniques or tactics.

333. Witch hunt

A "witch hunt" refers to a campaign based on unfounded or exaggerated accusations, often targeting a specific group or individual. This phrase comes from the historical practice of hunting and punishing people accused of practicing witchcraft, which occurred in Europe and later in America from the 15th to 18th centuries. During these hunts, individuals, often women on the fringes of society, were accused of causing misfortunes through magic and were imprisoned or tortured. Sometimes, they were even executed without the opportunity to defend themselves against the allegations. The expression is used in a negative or critical way today, implying that the campaign or pursuit is unfair or unjust. It was first used idiomatically in the United States in the 1940s and is still commonly used today to describe situations where people are targeted or pursued based on unfounded accusations.

334. Not all it's cracked up to be

The expression "not all it's cracked up to be" has its origins in an archaic meaning of the verb "crack," which was used to describe excessive boasting. This usage of "to crack" was prevalent during the late 18th and early 19th centuries. The phrase suggests that if something is touted as being superior, and subsequently fails to live up to that reputation, it can be said to not be all it's cracked up to be. This idiomatic expression is exemplified in the quote from the American frontiersman and politician Davy Crockett, who stated, "Martin Van Buren is not the man he is cracked up to be."

335. A class act

To be "a class act" means that a person is of high quality or that they demonstrate good manners, taste, or style. The phrase probably originated in the mid-20th century in the context of the entertainment industry, particularly in theater and movies. The expression is often used to praise individuals who have a strong sense of style, elegance, and professionalism, and are gracious, considerate, and well-mannered, treating others with respect and courtesy. It is also used to describe a performance, an event, or a product that is of high quality and well-executed. To understand the root of this idiom, it's important to consider the evolution of the word "class." In the 17th century, the term "class" was used to define status within a divided society. This use of the word is still common today, accompanied by the terms "higher," "middle," "lower," and "working." It wasn't until 1874 that the definition gained new usage in print, when John Hotten's Dictionary defined "class" as "The highest quality or combination of highest qualities among athletes."

336. Snug as a bug in a rug

The idiom "snug as a bug in a rug" refers to a situation in which someone is comfortable, warm, and secure, often in reference to being in bed or wrapped in a blanket. It is thought to have originated in the 19th century and is likely derived from the idea of a bug or insect being warm and secure inside a rug or blanket. Now, the phrase is used more broadly to describe any situation in which someone is comfortable, whether it is at home in bed or simply feeling at ease in a social or work setting. The expression is a common idiom in English and is often used to convey a sense of relaxation or contentment.

The phrase "a little bird told me" is used to describe information that has been obtained through insider knowledge or through hearing something from an unknown source. The idiom originated in the early 20th century and is often used as a metaphor for a confidential source of information. However, an alternative theory suggests that it may have been derived from the use of messenger birds and pigeons. Additionally, in Norse legend, Sigurd could hear and understand the birds after he slayed the dragon Fafnir, where the birds warned him that Regin would kill him.

338. A penny saved is a penny earned

"A penny saved is a penny earned" is used to express the idea that saving money is just as valuable as earning it. The phrase is believed to have originated in the 18th century and is often attributed to Benjamin Franklin, who included a similar saying in his 1737 book, *Poor Richard's Almanack*. The expression is used to encourage thrift and financial responsibility, suggesting that saving money is just as important as working for it.

339. Actions speak louder than words

The saying "actions speak louder than words" means that what a person does is more important than what they say. It suggests that a person's actions give a better understanding of their true beliefs, goals, and character compared to their words. This proverb has been around for a long time and can be found in many languages. It was first recorded in English in 1736 in a piece called "Melancholy State of Province" and says, "Actions speak louder than words, and are more to be regarded."

340. Blue once a month

The expression "blue once a month" is used to describe a person who is prone to feeling sad or depressed. It is thought to have originated in the United States in the early 20th century and has been in use in the English language for many decades. The phrase likely comes from the concept of "the blues," a term used to describe a feeling of sadness or melancholy. It is possible that the idiom "blue once a month" was originally used to describe someone who experienced these feelings on a regular, possibly monthly basis. Today, the phrase is used more broadly to describe someone who is prone to feeling sad or depressed, regardless of how often these feelings occur. It's often used in a casual or lighthearted manner, implying that the person's feelings of sadness are not particularly severe or persistent.

Did You Know?

- The word "set" has the highest number of definitions in the English language, with over 430. It can be used as a noun, verb, adjective, or adverb and can mean anything from a group of objects to a direction in which something is placed.
- The word "run" is the most common verb in the English language and it can be used in a wide range of contexts, including physical movement, the operation of a machine or system, and the performance of a task.
- The word "love" is the most common noun in the English language and it can refer to a variety of emotions, including affection, kindness, and attachment.
- The word "yoga" comes from the Sanskrit "yuj," which means "to yoke" or "to unite." It is a system of physical, mental, and spiritual practices that originated in ancient India and is designed to help achieve a state of balance and inner peace.
- The word "tattoo" comes from the Tahitian "tatau," which means "to mark."
- The word "ghoti" is a humorous way of illustrating the quirks of the English spelling system. It is pronounced "fish," but it is spelled using the "gh" from "enough," the "o" from "women," and the "ti" from "nation."

341. To bell the cat

"To bell the cat" means to take on a risky or dangerous task, especially one that is necessary but that others are unwilling to do. It often describes a situation where someone volunteers to do something that is difficult or risky, even though there is a possibility of failure or negative consequences. The origins of this idiom can be traced back to a fable about a group of mice who were being terrorized by a cat. The mice decided that they needed to find a way to protect themselves from the cat, and they came up with a plan to put a bell around the cat's neck so that they would always be able to hear it coming. However, when it came time to put the plan into action, none of the mice wanted to be the one to approach the cat and put the bell on it. The fable ends with the moral that it is easy to suggest solutions to problems, but it is much harder to actually take the necessary actions to solve them.

342. Dig one's heels in

The origins and history of the idiom "dig one's heels in" is rooted in the physical action of a person or animal resisting forward motion by leaning backwards and digging their heels into the ground. It is thought to have developed as a metaphor for someone who is stubborn or determined not to give in or change their stance on something. The phrase has been in use since the early 20th century and is commonly used to describe someone who is unwilling to compromise or budge on a particular issue.

343. The best thing since sliced bread

"The best thing since sliced bread" means something that is very good or innovative. It is often used to describe an invention that has made life easier or more convenient. The origin of this idiom is attributed to the invention of the bread-slicing machine in 1928. Before this time, bread was typically sold unsliced and had to be cut by hand. The bread-slicing machine made it much easier and more convenient to slice bread, and it became extremely popular.

344. Under the table

The expression "under the table" typically refers to something that is being done secretly or covertly. It can also mean something that is being done illegally or in violation of the rules or laws, such as in bribery or kickbacks. The phrase comes from the image of people passing money under a table so that others cannot see the exchange. This idiom has been in use since the mid-1900s.

345. Not your cup of tea

The idiom "not your cup of tea" is a metaphor that refers to the idea that everyone has different tastes and preferences, just like how people might prefer different types of tea. It is often used to politely decline an offer or suggestion, indicating that something is not to one's liking. The phrase is thought to have originated in Britain at the beginning of the 20th century, although the affirmative version (meaning something is to one's liking) was already in use at least as far back as the mid 18th century. The phrase "a cup of tea" was originally used to describe a favored friend. The expression was first used by the working class and became more widely known after appearing in William de Morgan's 1908 novel *Somehow Good*. By 1932, the expression was well-known enough to be used in Nancy Mitford's comic novel *Christmas Pudding* without any need for explanation.

346. To get on like a house on fire

"To get on like a house on fire" means to get along very well or to have a strong and harmonious relationship. It originated in the 19th century and may have originally been used to describe the idea of two people or groups forming a close relationship. In modern usage, the phrase commonly describes situations where two people or groups are able to communicate effectively and form a strong bond. It suggests that two people or groups have a strong and positive connection with one another, and are able to communicate and cooperate effectively as a result. It's thought to have been inspired by the idea of a house that is on fire, which suggests a situation that is intense or passionate.

347. Close, but no cigar

The idiom "close, but no cigar" describes a situation where someone comes close to achieving something but ultimately falls short of success. It is believed that the origin of the phrase can be traced back to the mid-20th century in the United States, when carnival exhibitions would offer cigars as rewards. Players had to win a game to receive a cigar, and those who came close but didn't win would be told "close, but no cigar" or "nice try, but no cigar." The phrase has since been used in various contexts, usually in a lighthearted and humorous way to describe someone who has come close but hasn't quite achieved success.

348. No horse in the race

The phrase "no horse in the race" (and no dog in the fight) means to have no stake or interest in a particular event or outcome. The phrase originated from horse racing, where each competitor is represented by a horse. If someone had no horse in the race, it means they have no horse competing and therefore no stake in the outcome. It's often used in a more general sense to indicate a lack of involvement or interest in a situation. This idiom has been used in print since the late 19th century.

349. Under the weather

The expression "under the weather" refers to a temporary state of feeling unwell. It has its origins in nautical terminology, where it was used to describe sailors who had become ill or seasick due to the harsh weather conditions at sea. To recover, these sailors were typically sent to the most stable part of the ship, which was located under the weather rail. The phrase conveys the idea that the individual is affected by the weather, and it was used to describe a variety of symptoms associated with seasickness, including nausea, dizziness, and a general feeling of malaise. It is important to note that the expression is not limited to describing physical illness, it can also be used to express a more general feeling of depression.

350. Good things come to those who wait

"Good things come to those who wait" is an idiom that means that positive outcomes will eventually be achieved by those who are patient and persistent. It originated in the 16th century and was inspired by the idea that good things often require time and effort to achieve, and that those who are willing to wait and put in the necessary effort will eventually be rewarded. In modern usage, the phrase is often used to encourage patience and perseverance and to keep working towards the goals, even when faced with challenges or setbacks.

Did You Know?

The Canterbury Tales is a collection of stories written in Middle English by Geoffrey Chaucer in the late 14th century. It is widely considered one of the greatest works of English literature and a cornerstone of medieval storytelling.

The Canterbury Tales consists of twenty-four tales, each told by a different narrator who is part of a group of travelers making a pilgrimage to the shrine of Thomas Becket in Canterbury, England. The stories range in genre from bawdy anecdotes and courtly love tales to moral allegories and religious narratives.

Each tale is unique in style, tone, and subject matter, offering a diverse representation of medieval society. Chaucer's depiction of his characters is vivid and engaging, showcasing their personalities, motivations, and flaws. The narrator of each tale reflects their own social status, upbringing, and education, providing insight into the cultural and literary traditions of the time.

One of the most famous tales in the collection is "The Knight's Tale," a chivalric romance that recounts the story of two knights who fall in love with the same woman. Another well-known tale is "The Wife of Bath's Tale," which tells the story of a bawdy woman who educates her fifth husband on the true nature of women.

In addition to its literary significance, *The Canterbury Tales* is also considered a landmark in the history of the English language. Chaucer's use of Middle English, a transitional stage between Old and Modern English, makes the tales accessible to modern readers while preserving the flavor of medieval language and culture.

351. Turn a deaf ear

To "turn a deaf ear" means to refuse to listen or pay attention. It is often used to describe a situation in which one intentionally ignores a request or suggestion, or fails to listen to what someone else is saying. The phrase was first recorded in the early 1400s by Walter Hylton, who wrote, "Make deef ere to hem as though thou herde hem not." Since then, versions of the expression have appeared in many proverb collections, from John Heywood's collection in 1546 to James Kelly's collection in 1721.

352. Fish story

"Fish story" is a term that refers to a tall tale or an exaggerated account. It originated with fishermen, who were known for telling humorous or entertaining stories about the size or number of fish that they had caught, even if those stories weren't entirely true. In modern usage, the phrase is often utilized more broadly to describe any exaggerated story, regardless of whether it's related to fishing. It's often used to gently tease or mock someone who is telling an unbelievable story as a way to suggest that the story may not be entirely factual or accurate. Overall, "fish story" is a playful way to describe a story that may be exaggerated or not entirely accurate.

353. Flesh and blood

The origin of the phrase "flesh and blood" can be traced back to the early translation of the Bible into Old English. Specifically, it appears in the Anglo-Saxon Gospels, Matthew 16:17, which was written around 1000 AD. The term in Old English is "hit ye ne onwreah flaesc ne blod," which was later translated in the King James Bible as "Flesh and blood hath not revealed it unto thee." By the time Shakespeare arrived on the scene, "flesh and blood" had already become a commonly-used phrase and its meaning was well established. The idiom emphasizes the human condition and how we are all just frail, biological beings.

354. To be on the same wavelength

"To be on the same wavelength" means to be in agreement or to have a shared understanding. It originated in the early 20th century and described the idea that two people or groups are able to understand one another's thoughts or intentions. The phrase is thought to have been inspired by the concept of radio waves, which are used to transmit and receive information, and the idea that two radios that are "tuned" to the same frequency will be able to communicate with one another. In modern usage, it suggests that two people or groups have a shared perspective on something, and are able to communicate effectively because of that shared understanding.

355. Every nook and cranny

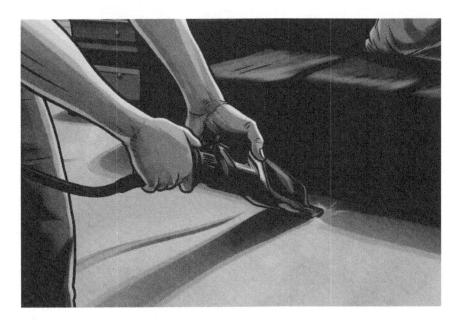

The idiom "every nook and cranny" has been utilized since the early 19th century and refers to thoroughly searching every small or concealed location. The phrase is thought to have originated from the maritime term "nook," denoting a small corner or alcove, and "cranny," meaning a tiny fissure or crevice. Both of these terms have been in use since the 14th century. The earliest documented occurrence of the idiom can be found in the 1803 publication of the book *Scottish Scenery* by James Cririe, in which the following verse is written: "The piercing frost, the mass of drifted snow, that smooths the valley with the higher ridge, and ev'ry winding nook and cranny fills?"

356. Eat like a bird

The idiomatic phrase "eat like a bird" is used to describe someone who eats very little, usually referring to a small or dainty person. The expression originated in the early 20th century and likely refers to the small size and delicate eating habits of birds. However, this simile alludes to the mistaken impression that birds don't eat much (they actually do, relative to their size), and dates from the first half of the 1900s. An antonym of this phrase is "eat like a horse," which dates from the early 1700s, and alludes to the tendency of horses to eat whatever food is available. This idiom is used to describe someone who eats a lot or eats in large quantities.

357. Straw that broke the camel's back

The famous idiom "the straw that broke the camel's back" refers to a small, seemingly insignificant event or action that, when added to a series of previous events, causes a situation to become unbearable or a problem to become insurmountable. It is often used to describe a circumstance where someone has been subjected to a series of small, incremental stresses or difficulties, and the final straw is the one that causes them to snap or reach their breaking point. The origin of the phrase can be traced back to ancient times and the practice of camel caravans in the Middle East. Camels are capable of carrying heavy loads, but their backs are not designed to withstand an infinite amount of weight. If a camel's back is already loaded with a heavy pack, and then an additional straw is added, it can cause the camel's back to give out. This idiom was first recorded in print in the 18th century.

358. Bounce something off someone

The expression "bounce something off someone" means to discuss something informally, usually to get another person's opinion or feedback. It is often used as a way to test out an idea or get someone's perspective on a matter before making a decision or taking further action. The phrase suggests the idea of tossing an idea or question back and forth between people in order to get different viewpoints and insights. The metaphor underlying this idiom was described in a 1956 newspaper, which stated that ideas have a lot in common with rubber balls, in that the way they bounce depends on various factors such as the starting point, the force with which they were thrown, the character of the surface they hit, and the ambient temperature. All of these factors can influence the bounce of a ball and the rebound of an idea. This idiom is often used in a casual or informal setting, such as when brainstorming ideas or seeking advice from a colleague or friend.

359. We'll cross that bridge when we get to it

"We'll cross that bridge when we get to it" means that one will deal with a problem or issue when it arises, rather than worrying about it in advance. It is often used as a way to reassure someone or to indicate that there is no need to worry about something until it becomes necessary. Even though the origin of the phrase is not known, it has been utilized since before the 1800s when long travels were done on foot or horseback and crossing bridges was a common occurrence. The reliability of faraway bridges was not guaranteed, so crossing a bridge was considered a risky matter and a metaphor for solving problems. The adverb "when" indicates that the event is anticipated to take place in the future, while the conjunction "if" introduces a conditional clause, indicating that the event is not inevitable. The first recorded use of the idiom can be found in Henry Wadsworth Longfellow's *The Golden Legend* (1851): "Don't cross the bridge till you come to it, is a proverb old and of excellent wit." The phrase is often changed to "I'll cross that bridge if I come to it."

360. Don't rain on my parade

The idiom "rain on someone's parade" means to spoil or ruin someone's plans or enjoyment. The phrase is typically used as a verb, as in "Don't rain on my parade," which means "Don't try to spoil my plans or enjoyment of something." It can also be used as a noun, as in "She was a real rain on the parade." The expression frequently describes someone who is overly critical or pessimistic and has a tendency to bring others down. The saying is thought to have originated in the United States in the early 20th century and is said colloquially in a lighthearted or humorous way. One theory is that it refers to the tradition of parades, which are often held outdoors and are subject to the weather. If it starts to rain during a parade, it can ruin the event and dampen the mood of the participants and spectators. Another theory is that it is derived from the phrase "pour cold water on," which means to spoil or ruin something.

Did You Know?

J.K. Rowling's *Harry Potter* series has taken the literary world by storm, enchanting readers of all ages with its magical storytelling. The first book in the series, *Harry Potter and the Sorcerer's Stone*, has been sold a hundred and twenty million copies. It introduces readers to the young wizard Harry Potter as he embarks on a journey of self-discovery and battles against the forces of darkness. This modern fantasy classic has captured the hearts of readers globally, fostering a community of fans and igniting a renewed interest in reading among young audiences.

Don Quixote by Miguel de Cervantes is a literary masterpiece that has captured the imagination of readers for centuries. This novel follows the adventures of the delusional yet endearing Don Quixote as he tilts at windmills and quests for chivalrous ideals. Renowned for its wit, satire, and exploration of the nature of reality, *Don Quixote* laid the foundation for modern fiction and remains a beloved classic that has inspired countless works of literature. This novel has sold over five hundred million copies.

The Bible stands as one of the most popular and influential books of all time, shaping the beliefs, ethics, and cultures of millions around the world. Its stories, teachings, and historical accounts have provided guidance and inspiration for generations, impacting art, literature, and even political thought. The Bible continues to be a source of spiritual and moral insight, making it an enduring cornerstone of human literature. The Bible has sold anywhere between five and seven billion copies.

These three books – *Harry Potter and the Sorcerer's Stone*, *Don Quixote*, and The Bible – have each left an indelible mark on the literary landscape, captivating readers and influencing the way stories are told and experienced.

361. Take a rain check

The saying "take a rain check" is used to indicate that one will accept a future opportunity instead of the current one that is being offered. The phrase originated in the late 19th century from the world of baseball, where a "rain check" was a ticket that could be used to attend a game that was rained out, and thus, could not be completed. The expression is often used in the context of social invitations or events, where one can't attend the event but would like to attend the next time. It's a polite way of declining an invitation without offending the host. The idiom is also commonly used in the context of shopping or buying products, when the item is out of stock and the customer can't purchase it, they can take a rain check and buy it later.

362. Shoot oneself in the foot

To "shoot oneself in the foot" means to harm or sabotage oneself, often through one's own actions or words. It is often used to describe someone who is their own worst enemy or who unintentionally causes problems or setbacks. The phrase originates from a phenomenon that became common during the First World War, when soldiers would shoot themselves in the foot in order to be sent to the hospital tent rather than being sent into battle, claiming the shooting to be accidental. The metaphor suggests that one is causing problems or setbacks for oneself, much like these soldiers were causing harm to themselves in order to avoid battle. The earliest written use of this expression dates back to the early 20th century. It appears in *The American Language* by H.L. Mencken, which was published in 1919.

363. Hold your horses

The idiom "hold your horses" is thought to have come from the United States during the 1800s. Originally, it was written as "hold your hosses," using the American slang term "hoss" for a horse. The phrase is used to tell someone to be patient or to wait a moment before acting or speaking. It is believed to have originated from horse racing, where a jockey would tell their horse to "hold" or "stay" when waiting for the starting signal. Additionally, it could also have roots in the military as a command to stop or wait before proceeding. The expression took its current form in 1939.

364. Raise one's hackles

To "raise one's hackles" means to become defensive or aggressive, often as a result of feeling threatened or offended. The phrase originated in the 19th century and it comes from the physical reaction of certain animals, such as dogs, when they feel threatened or aggressive. When animals feel threatened, their body hair (or hackles) will stand up, making them appear larger and more intimidating. This physical reaction is known as "raising the hackles," and it is thought to be a sign of aggression or defensiveness. The idiom is often used to describe human behavior as well, particularly when someone becomes aggressive in response to a perceived offense or danger.

365. Don't put all your eggs in one basket

The expression "don't put all your eggs in one basket" is used as a warning against putting all of one's resources into a single venture or relying too heavily on one thing. The phrase suggests that if all of one's eggs, or resources, are placed into a single basket, and that basket is lost or destroyed, all of the eggs (resources) will be lost as well. This idiom comes from an old proverb, most likely Spanish or Italian, and was first found in print during the 17th century. The phrase appears in *Don Quixote* by Miguel de Cervantes in 1615 who wrote, "It is the part of a wise man to keep himself today for tomorrow, and not venture all his eggs in one basket." It's also found in *A Common Place of Italian Proverbs and Proverbial Phrases* by Giovanni Torriano in 1666 and is similar to an older proverb, originally in Latin: "Venture not all in one ship."

366. Between a rock and a hard place

"Between a rock and a hard place" is used to describe a situation in which someone is faced with two difficult or undesirable options and is unable to choose between them. It suggests that they are in a difficult or impossible predicament, and that either choice they make will have negative consequences. The origin of this phrase can be traced back to early 1900s America and a dispute between copper miners and mining companies in Arizona. The miners sought better working conditions and the companies refused to provide. This created a dilemma for the miners, who were faced with two unsavory options: endure the same grueling conditions (a rock), or face unemployment and poverty (a hard place). The idiom gained widespread usage during the Great Depression of the 1930s, as many individuals found themselves in a similar situation, caught between a rock and a hard place, due to the dire economic conditions of the time.

367. Sit on the fence

To "sit on the fence" refers to a neutral or impartial stance in a situation, characterized by the avoidance of taking a side or making a decision. The origin of this phrase is uncertain, but it is believed to have emerged in the late 19th century. One theory suggests that the expression is derived from the image of a person physically sitting on a fence, which serves as a barrier that separates two sides. This metaphor implies that the person is neither choosing a side nor making a decision. Another theory posits that it may have originated from the practice of people sitting on fences to observe disputes or arguments without becoming involved. This behavior, known as "spectating," is thought to have influenced the adoption of the idiom to describe a similar behavior in human interactions.

368. To cut someone some slack

The idiom "cut someone some slack" is an informal expression that means to be understanding and forgiving towards a person, and to give them some leeway or understanding. It is often used to encourage someone to relax or not be too hard on themselves or others. This expression originated around the mid-1900s and is thought to allude to the slackening of tautness in a rope or sail. The word "slack" has a rich history, with its earliest known usage dating back to the 1300s. In this time, the word meant cessation of pain or grief. However, the idiom "cut someone some slack" does not come from this definition of the word. Instead, it comes from the word's other definition, which refers to the loose part of a sail or rope. This definition dates back to the late-1700s.

369. Spice things up

To "spice things up" means to make something more interesting, exciting, or lively. It can be used in many different contexts, such as in a relationship, a conversation, a party, or a situation that has become monotonous. The phrase is thought to have originated from the use of spices in cooking, where a spice is a substance added to food or drink to intensify the flavor. Spices are usually aromatic and robust to the taste and many spices are well known to have medicinal or alchemical properties. The word "spice" comes from Latin, "species" (plural) meaning "spices, goods, wares" and in classical Latin, it meant "kind, sort." In Old French it was written as "espice" and the modern version modified it to "épice." The expression "to spice things up" emerged as a figurative meaning, since the nature of herbs was used to improve the flavor and enjoyment of food. This meaning is believed to have originated around the 1520s.

370. To get a second wind

The expression "to get a second wind" suggests that a person is able to find an additional source of energy or strength, as if they are able to take a deep breath and keep going. It usually refers to a scenario where someone is able to overcome a challenge or obstacle by finding a renewed sense of energy or determination. This idiom has been in use since the late 1800s and originally referred to the return of a regular breathing pattern after any kind of physical effort. Long-distance runners often do get a "second wind" at some point in a race when they find it easier to breathe. In *The Franchise Affair* (1946), Josephine Tey wrote: "Perhaps it was the presence of an ally… or perhaps she had just got her second wind."

Did You Know?

The Great Barrier Reef, located off the coast of Australia, is the world's largest coral reef system, stretching over 1,400 miles (2,253 kilometers). This incredible ecosystem is composed of thousands of individual reefs and islands, offering a home to an astonishing diversity of marine life, including vibrant coral formations, tropical fish, sharks, and sea turtles. The Great Barrier Reef is a UNESCO World Heritage Site and is recognized for its ecological significance and global importance. However, it is also under threat due to factors such as coral bleaching caused by rising sea temperatures.

The Tower of Pisa, known worldwide for its distinctive tilt, is a freestanding bell tower located in Pisa, Italy. The tower's construction began in the 12th century and was characterized by a foundation sinking into the soft ground, leading to its iconic lean. It stands at about 186 feet (fifty-six meters) tall and consists of several stories adorned with intricate white marble designs. Despite its unintended tilt, the Tower of Pisa has become a symbol of architectural curiosity and draws millions of visitors from around the globe.

Mount Everest, Earth's highest mountain, reaches an elevation of 29,032 feet (8,849 meters) above sea level. Situated in the Himalayas between Nepal and China, its towering peak has captivated the imaginations of climbers and adventurers for decades. Scaling Mount Everest is a challenging and dangerous feat due to extreme altitudes, unpredictable weather, and treacherous conditions. The mountain's allure, however, persists, and the region has become a focal point for mountaineering expeditions and exploration.

371. Elbow grease

The term "elbow grease" refers to the physical effort and hard work that is required to complete a task or achieve a goal. It is often used to describe the effort that is needed to clean or maintain something, such as scrubbing a floor or polishing a car. The phrase suggests that one must be willing to put in a lot of hard work and exert themselves in order to get a job done, and that this may involve using one's hands and arms to apply force or pressure. The idiom is thought to have originated in the early 19th century and it may have come from the idea of using one's elbow to apply force or pressure when scrubbing or cleaning. The phrase is commonly said as encouragement for someone to work hard and to persevere even when a task is difficult.

372. Smoke and mirrors

The idiom "smoke and mirrors" describes a situation where deception or manipulation is used to create an illusion or distract attention from the truth. The phrase originated from the world of stage magic and illusion, where smoke and mirrors were used to create the illusion of objects appearing or disappearing. The technique was first documented as early as 1770 and became popular after its use by the charlatan Johann Georg Schröpfer. It was a staple in 19th-century phantasmagoria shows. Phantasmagoria was a genre of horror theater that employed the use of one or multiple magic lanterns to cast haunting images, including skeletons, demons, and ghosts onto walls, smoke, or translucent screens. The illusion was achieved through the utilization of a secret projector, referred to as a magic lantern, which projected light through a mirror and into a cloud of smoke, dispersing the beam and producing the image.

373. Give them a run for their money

The phrase "give them a run for their money" describes the act of competing fiercely or giving a strong effort in a competition or challenge. It originated in the early 20th century and comes from horse racing. If a horse is withdrawn from a race, past a certain point, the punters who have bet on it lose their money, which makes the trainer, the stable, and the owner very unpopular with the betting public. In order to avoid this, the trainer may keep a horse that is not at its best in the race, giving the backers "a run for their money" even if the chances of winning are poor. The first recorded use of this expression in this context was in 1874.

374. See a man about a dog

The idiom "see a man about a dog" or "see a man about a horse" is used as a polite or evasive way of saying that one needs to leave or go somewhere without providing a specific reason. The phrase is often used as a way of excusing oneself from a conversation or situation without giving any details about where one is going or what one is doing. The first recorded usage of this idiom can be traced back to the play *Flying Scud* written by Dion Boucicault in 1866, in which a character employs the phrase as a means of nonchalantly avoiding a problematic situation, stating, "Excuse me Mr. Quail, I cannot linger; I must attend to a matter concerning a canine." It is believed that the idiom "see a man about a dog" was originally utilized to refer to the act of procuring or disposing of a dog, which was considered a routine and unremarkable task. Analogously, "see a man about a horse" is thought to have alluded to the act of purchasing or disposing of a horse.

375. Get off your high horse

When telling someone to "get off their high horse," you ask them to stop acting so pompous. One of the earliest uses of the term is from 1380 in John Wyclif's English Works, "Ye emperour...made hym & his cardenals ride in reed on hye ors." The line refers to warhorses, which were immense, powerful creatures. The higher up in military ranks a person was, the bigger their horse would be to announce the status of the rider visually. Despite its mention in the late 1300s, the metaphorical phrase came into use in the mid-to-late 1700s.

376. Scratch someone's back

The phrase "to scratch someone's back" is an idiomatic expression that refers to a mutually beneficial relationship. It describes a situation where one does a favor or provides help for someone in exchange for the expectation that the person will do the same for them in the future. The origins of the phrase are rooted in the English Navy during the 1600s. During this time, a punishment for crew members involved being tied to the mast and lashed. To ease the severity of this punishment, the crew members would make a deal among themselves to deliver light lashes, effectively just "scratching the offender's back." The shortened version of this expression was first recorded in 1704.

377. Put something on the map

To "put something on the map" refers to making something known or famous, bringing attention to it, or making it a popular destination or topic. It originated in the early 1900s, and it comes from the idea of marking a location on a map to show that it is known or important. The phrase alludes to the idea that something or someone that was previously unknown or insignificant has become famous. It was first used to describe a town or city that had grown to the point that it is important enough to be included on a map. This could be in terms of population, economic activity, or other factors that make it a significant location.

378. Scrape the barrel

The expression "scrape the barrel" refers to a situation where the available options or resources are of low quality or are running out. It originated in the 19th century when barrels were used to store and transport goods, and "scraping the barrel" meant scooping out the last remnants of a substance from the bottom. Now, the phrase is often used figuratively to describe a situation where the available options or resources are limited or low quality. It's often used to convey a sense of desperation or a lack of alternatives.

379. A watched pot never boils

The idiom "a watched pot never boils" conveys the impatience we often feel when waiting for something to happen. It suggests that when we're anxiously monitoring a process, time seems to crawl by, making the anticipated event feel even more distant. The saying's origins can be traced back to the 16th century, when cooking was more laborious and required constant attention. While its first written use isn't precisely documented, the phrase's essence has endured. In modern times, it's used beyond the kitchen, serving as a reminder that incessantly waiting for something can make it feel slower to arrive. Today, we invoke this idiom to encourage a more patient outlook, reminding ourselves and others that allowing events to unfold naturally can ultimately make the wait more bearable and the outcome sweeter.

380. Between the devil and the deep blue sea

The idiom "between the devil and the deep blue sea" paints a vivid picture of being caught in a difficult, no-win situation with two equally undesirable options. This maritime-inspired expression has its origins in the nautical world, where sailors faced the treacherous choice of staying aboard a ship plagued by an oncoming storm ("the devil") or jumping into the uncertain depths of the open ocean ("the deep blue sea"). While the phrase's earliest recorded use in writing dates back to the 17th century, its metaphorical resonance remains potent. Today, it's a captivating way to describe being stuck between unfavorable alternatives, capturing the tension and anxiety of navigating life's tough decisions.

Did You Know?

Located in Mecca, Saudi Arabia, the Abraj Al Bait Clock Tower reaches a height of 1,972 feet (601 meters), securing its place as the third tallest building in the world. Part of a complex surrounding the Masjid al-Haram, Islam's holiest mosque, this tower serves as a symbol of the city's spiritual significance. Its distinct clock faces and ornate architectural elements not only provide functional features but also reflect the intricate craftsmanship of the region. The Abraj Al Bait Clock Tower stands as a remarkable fusion of modernity and tradition.

Rising in the heart of Shanghai, China, the Shanghai Tower reaches a remarkable height of 2,073 feet (632 meters), making it the second tallest building globally. This unique skyscraper features a twisting design that not only offers striking aesthetics but also enhances its structural stability in the face of high winds. Housing commercial spaces, hotels, and observation decks, the Shanghai Tower exemplifies China's rapid urban development and commitment to cutting-edge design principles.

The Burj Khalifa in Dubai, United Arab Emirates, stands as the world's tallest building, soaring to a staggering height of 2,722 feet (828 meters). This architectural marvel dominates the city's skyline with its sleek design and state-of-the-art engineering. Its multi-use structure includes residential spaces, offices, and luxurious amenities, showcasing the epitome of modern skyscraper innovation. The Burj Khalifa's towering presence is a testament to human ingenuity and the pursuit of pushing architectural boundaries.

381. Bite the hand that feeds you

The idiom "bite the hand that feeds you" conveys the notion of acting ungratefully or disrespectfully towards someone who has provided support, help, or resources. Imagine a scenario where a dog, instead of appreciating the hand that offers food, responds by biting it. This powerful imagery illustrates the idea that turning against those who aid us can be both foolish and detrimental. The origins of this expression can be traced back to classical literature, with various forms appearing in works like Aesop's fables. Its earliest recorded use in its modern form dates back to the 17th century, in a play by John Heywood. Over time, its meaning has maintained its potency, serving as a timeless reminder to acknowledge and appreciate those who assist us, and cautioning against undermining our own support systems through ingratitude. Today, we still invoke this idiom to counsel against harming relationships by failing to recognize the value of assistance or favor.

382. By the book

The idiom "by the book" encapsulates the idea of strictly adhering to established rules, protocols, or guidelines. This phrase reflects a commitment to doing things in a methodical and conventional manner, prioritizing conformity over innovation. Its origins trace back to the military, where regulations were outlined in official manuals or "books." While its earliest use isn't definitively documented, it appeared in writings as early as the 19th century. Over time, its meaning has broadened beyond the military realm to encompass any situation where adherence to predetermined procedures takes precedence. Today, "by the book" is employed to describe someone who sticks closely to the rules, often invoking a balance between efficiency and creativity or highlighting the contrast between strict adherence and flexible thinking.

383. Keep your chin up

The idiom "keep your chin up" serves as a resilient reminder to maintain a positive attitude, even in the face of challenges. Think of it as lifting your head high, almost as if you're defying adversity with a determined spirit. The phrase finds its roots in the world of boxing, where a fighter is encouraged to keep their chin up to avoid being hit. Its earliest recorded appearance in writing can be traced back to the late 19th century. Over time, the meaning has expanded beyond physical posture to embrace emotional resilience. Today, we use this expression as a supportive gesture, offering encouragement to friends or colleagues facing tough times. It's a warm nudge to stay strong, reminding us that even in the midst of difficulty, maintaining a hopeful outlook can make a significant difference.

384. Make hay while the sun shines

The idiom "make hay while the sun shines" encapsulates the wisdom of seizing opportunities when they're presented, just as farmers harvest hay during sunny weather to ensure its quality. It's like capturing the essence of acting when conditions are ideal for success. This phrase originated in agrarian (agricultural) societies, reflecting the practicality of capitalizing on good weather for efficient crop harvesting. While its exact first use in writing isn't precisely known, it emerged in the English language during the 16th century. As time has progressed, its significance has grown beyond farming to encapsulate the broader idea of not procrastinating when circumstances are favorable. In modern times, we use "make hay while the sun shines" as a motivational reminder to act promptly and decisively, ensuring that we don't miss out on promising opportunities that come our way.

385. Not a snowball's chance in hell

The idiom "not a snowball's chance in hell" captures the essence of utter impossibility, conveying the idea that something has virtually no chance of happening. It's like suggesting that a snowball could survive in the searing heat of the netherworld. This fiery expression likely has roots in the religious imagery of eternal damnation and began to appear in literature in the 19th century. Over time, the phrase has evolved from a purely theological context to a more colloquial one, describing situations where success or achievement is incredibly unlikely. Today, we use it to humorously emphasize the extreme improbability of an event, adding a dash of fiery rhetoric to our conversations about the improbable and the impossible.

386. Out of the frying pan and into the fire

The idiom "out of the frying pan and into the fire" paints a vivid image of moving from a challenging situation to an even worse one. It's like escaping the heat of a frying pan only to find oneself in the midst of flames. This expression draws from the realm of cooking and dates back to the medieval times, when fire and frying pans were integral to daily life. Its first recorded use in writing was in John Heywood's 1546 work, "Proverbes," revealing its deep historical roots. Over time, its meaning has broadened beyond the literal context to describe any unfortunate transition from one difficulty to another. Today, the idiom offers a poetic and succinct way to convey the idea that sometimes, our attempts to escape trouble can lead us into more trouble, a cautionary tale woven into our conversations about navigating life's challenges.

387. Read someone like a book

The idiom "read someone like a book" captures the idea of understanding someone's thoughts, emotions, or intentions with remarkable ease, much like flipping through the pages of a well-worn book. It's a metaphorical lens into human perception and insight. While its exact origins remain elusive, the expression's roots can be traced back to the 19th century, a time when books were integral to culture and communication. The idiom's first known use in writing appeared in the 1920s. Over time, it has evolved from a literal connection to books to encompass a broader understanding of human behavior. Today, we use this expression playfully and conversationally, often to highlight our ability to decipher nonverbal cues, motives, or emotions, and sometimes to acknowledge the depth of our relationships or our perceptive acumen in social situations.

388. The devil you know is better than the devil you don't

The idiom "the devil you know is better than the devil you don't" encapsulates the notion that sticking with a familiar, albeit undesirable, situation is often preferable to venturing into an unknown, potentially worse one. It's a pithy reminder that the risks of change can sometimes outweigh the discomfort of the familiar. Its origins can be traced to the 16th century, with variations appearing in various languages. While its first recorded use in writing isn't pinpointed, it resonates with timeless wisdom. Over time, the phrase has expanded beyond its original context, offering guidance on risk assessment and decision-making. Today, we invoke it to consider the pros and cons of new endeavors, acknowledging that while familiarity might breed discontent, navigating the unknown carries its own set of uncertainties, a piece of sagacious advice often shared when weighing the potential outcomes of challenging choices.

389. The shoe is on the other foot

The idiom "the shoe is on the other foot" playfully captures the essence of role reversal, indicating a situation where circumstances have shifted, often resulting in a complete change of perspective or fortune. It's like swapping shoes with someone, suddenly experiencing life from their vantage point. With its origins in the 19th century, its exact first use in writing isn't definitively known. However, the phrase's metaphorical appeal has remained consistent. Over time, its meaning has expanded to symbolize any situation where power dynamics or expectations have been inverted. Today, we use this idiom to highlight the amusing or thought-provoking aspects of changing fortunes or altered positions, adding a touch of wit to conversations about shifts in roles, power, or circumstances.

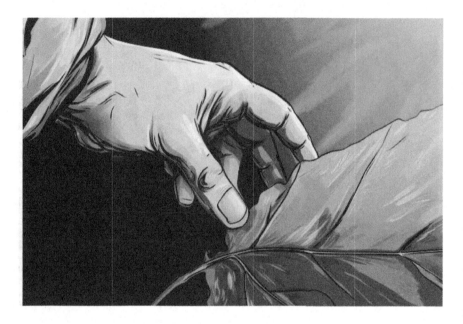

The idiom "turn over a new leaf" encapsulates the concept of making a fresh start or embracing a positive change in one's behavior or circumstances. It's like flipping to a blank page in the book of life, ready to rewrite the story. The phrase's origins can be traced back to the medieval times when books were made of leaves. While its exact first use in writing isn't precisely documented, it resonates with timeless self-improvement aspirations. Over time, the idiom has evolved from a literal reference to books to encompass personal growth and transformation. Today, this expression is used to encourage or acknowledge positive shifts in habits, attitudes, or situations, imbuing conversations with a hopeful and motivational undertone, reminding ourselves and others that change is always possible and rejuvenating.

Did You Know?

The origin of languages is an enigmatic tale that unfolds across the vast expanse of human history. It's a story of our innate drive to communicate, connect, and make sense of the world around us. While the exact details remain shrouded in the depths of time, linguists and researchers have pieced together clues from diverse disciplines to offer insights into the birth of human languages.

At its core, language is a powerful tool that sets us apart from other species. The journey likely began with early humans using simple gestures, vocalizations, and mimicry to convey basic needs and emotions. Over time, this rudimentary communication system evolved in response to the growing complexity of human societies. Our ancestors found innovative ways to express abstract concepts, share knowledge, and build social bonds, leading to the emergence of structured language.

The development of language was intimately intertwined with our cognitive evolution. As our brains expanded in size and complexity, our ability to process and manipulate symbols also grew. This cognitive leap enabled the formation of intricate grammatical structures and the capacity for storytelling, which became essential for passing down cultural knowledge and shaping collective identities. Through a dynamic interplay of culture, cognition, and communication, languages blossomed into the rich tapestry of diversity we see today, each one a testament to humanity's remarkable journey of expression.

391. Walking on air

The idiom "walking on air" captures the exhilarating sensation of extreme happiness or euphoria, akin to floating above the ground. It's like feeling so elated that your feet barely touch the earth. The phrase's origins are rooted in the idea of weightlessness, tracing back to the early 20th century. While its exact first use in writing isn't definitively known, its imagery has carried through generations. Over time, "walking on air" has expanded beyond its literal connection to flying and levity, to encompass any scenario where sheer joy or contentment prevails. Today, we use the expression to depict the elation of accomplishment, romance, or positive life events, infusing conversations with an air of happiness that's almost palpable, a lightness that reflects the wonderful feeling of being on cloud nine.

392. Wear your heart on your sleeve

The idiom "wear your heart on your sleeve" paints a vivid picture of openness and vulnerability, suggesting that someone openly displays their emotions for all to see, much like a badge of honor or a symbol pinned to their sleeve. It's as if one's inner feelings are out there for the world to witness. The phrase's origins trace back to the Middle Ages, when knights wore their ladies' favor on their sleeves as a sign of devotion. While its first recorded use in writing isn't precisely documented, it appeared in Shakespeare's "Othello" in 1604, illuminating its longstanding resonance. Over time, the meaning has evolved to denote emotional transparency and authenticity. Today, we use this expresion to both praise and caution individuals who openly express their feelings, recognizing the courage it takes to do so while also highlighting the potential risks of emotional exposure.

393. When it rains, it pours

The idiom "when it rains, it pours" aptly captures the notion that challenges or difficulties often arrive in clusters, just as heavy rainfalls can suddenly intensify. It's as if life's obstacles gather momentum and pour down all at once. The origins of this expression can be traced back to a Morton Salt advertisement in the early 20th century, wherein the phrase was coined to describe the pouring ability of their salt even in humid conditions. This clever marketing has since become a part of our lexicon. Over time, the idiom's meaning has expanded to encompass various situations where multiple problems or occurrences arise simultaneously, overwhelming an individual or situation. Today, we use it to commiserate with others facing a series of challenges or to share our own experiences of navigating a flood of difficulties, acknowledging the unpredictable nature of life's ups and downs.

394. Zero in on something

The idiom "zero in on something" refers to the act of focusing intensely and precisely on a particular target or objective. It's like narrowing down your attention until you hit the bullseye with laser-like accuracy. The phrase's origins can be traced to the world of aviation and military technology during World War II, where pilots used radar technology to "zero in" on enemy targets. Its first documented use in writing dates back to the 1940s. Over time, the idiom's meaning has expanded to include any situation where one concentrates intently on a subject or goal. Today, it is used to describe a deliberate and sharp focus, whether it's in problem-solving, decision-making, or honing in on details. It's a powerful expression that encapsulates the precision and determination required to achieve one's aims.

395. Burning the candle at both ends

The idiom "burning the candle at both ends" portrays the image of someone exhausting themselves by working excessively or indulging in various activities without respite. It's as if the candle of one's energy is being consumed from both sides, rapidly depleting its light. This phrase's origins can be traced to the 18th century poem by Edmund Clerihew Bentley, where he mentioned "A man who's burning his candle at both ends." Over time, its meaning has expanded beyond its original poetic context to encompass any situation where someone is overextending themselves, often at the cost of their well-being. Today we use this expression to caution against excessive work, stress, or overcommitment, reminding ourselves and others of the importance of finding balance and preserving one's energy for sustainable success and health.

396. Count your blessings

The idiom "count your blessings" encapsulates the sage advice of taking a moment to appreciate and acknowledge the positive aspects of one's life, even in the midst of challenges. It's like stepping back to tally up the good fortune and joys that often go unnoticed. The phrase's origins can be traced to religious texts and teachings, emphasizing gratitude for life's gifts. Its earliest documented use in writing is in the 16th century, in Thomas Tallis' hymn "All praise to Thee, my God, this night." Over time, the idiom has evolved from its religious roots to a broader cultural context, urging individuals to recognize the silver linings and small victories in life. Today, it is used as a gentle reminder to shift our perspective, fostering an attitude of thankfulness and resilience in the face of adversity.

397. Every dog has its day

The idiom "every dog has its day" refers to the belief that everyone, regardless of their current circumstances, will experience a period of success, recognition, or triumph at some point in their life. It's like a reminder that even the most overlooked or underestimated individuals will eventually shine. The phrase's origins can be traced back to ancient Roman and Greek literature, where similar sentiments were expressed. Its first use in English literature dates back to the 16th century, appearing in John Heywood's collection of proverbs. Over time, the idiom has evolved from a proverbial expression to a broader motivational message, encouraging perseverance and offering hope during challenging times. Today, we use it to uplift others and ourselves, emphasizing that setbacks are temporary, and every person is capable of achieving their moment of success or recognition, regardless of their initial circumstances.

398. Fish or cut bait

The idiom "fish or cut bait" delivers a straightforward ultimatum: make a decision and take action, or step aside and let others proceed. The phrase's origins are deeply rooted in the world of fishing, where one either engages in the act of fishing or abandons the endeavor. Its earliest recorded use in writing dates back to the 19th century, reflecting its direct and practical essence. Over time, the meaning has expanded to signify the need for commitment and determination in any endeavor, highlighting the importance of taking responsibility for one's choices. Today, we use this idiom to motivate or challenge others to take decisive action, often in situations where indecision or hesitation is hindering progress. It's an expression that beckons individuals to take control of their destiny and contribute actively to their own success.

399. Hit the ground running

The idiom "hit the ground running" encapsulates the notion of starting a new endeavor with immediate and energetic action, as if you're already in full stride the moment you begin. It's like launching into a project with enthusiasm and momentum from the very start. The origins of this phrase are often attributed to the military, describing paratroopers who would jump from planes and immediately engage in combat upon landing. While its exact first use in writing isn't known, it gained prominence in the business world during the mid-20th century. Over time, its meaning has expanded beyond its military and business contexts to encompass any situation where one begins with vigor and readiness. Today, this expression to encourage a dynamic and proactive approach to new challenges, whether in work, sports, or life in general, underscoring the value of a strong and impactful beginning.

400. Keep something at bay

The idiom "keep something at bay" conjures the image of holding a threat or challenge at a distance, preventing it from getting too close or causing harm. The origins of this phrase can be traced back to hunting, where dogs would be kept at bay, or restrained, to prevent them from attacking prey until commanded. While its earliest written use is unclear, it emerged in common language during the 16th century. Over time, the meaning has broadened beyond its literal hunting context to encompass any situation where one is managing or controlling a potential problem or difficulty. Today, we use this phrase to efforts to ward off challenges or threats, underscoring the proactive strategies we employ to maintain control and ensure our safety and well-being.

Did You Know?

Shanghai, located in China, ranks as the third most populous city in the world, with a metropolitan population exceeding twenty-seven million people. This global financial center is renowned for its rapid development, cutting-edge architecture, and international influence. The city's historic waterfront, futuristic skyline, and economic significance make it a symbol of China's transformation on the world stage.

Delhi, India's capital territory, holds the distinction of being the second most populous city globally, with a metropolitan population surpassing thirty-one million people. With a rich historical heritage that spans centuries, Delhi is a city of contrasts, offering ancient monuments alongside modern skyscrapers. Its vibrant markets, religious sites, and cultural diversity contribute to its status as a thriving urban hub.

Tokyo, the capital city of Japan, stands as the most populous city in the world, with a population exceeding thirty-seven million people in its metropolitan area. This bustling metropolis is a center of culture, technology, and commerce, boasting a vibrant blend of tradition and innovation. Its efficient public transportation, diverse neighborhoods, and iconic landmarks reflect the dynamic nature of urban life on a massive scale.

These three densely populated cities – Shanghai, Delhi, and Tokyo – showcase the complexities of urban living on an unprecedented scale. Each city presents a unique blend of tradition and progress, illustrating the diverse ways in which societies adapt to accommodate the challenges and opportunities of modern urbanization.

401. Like shooting fish in a barrel

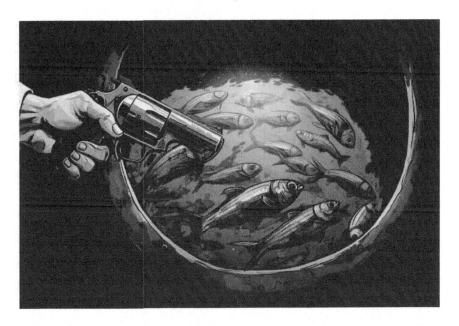

The idiom "like shooting fish in a barrel" refers to the idea of an exceptionally easy task or endeavor, as if you're aiming at fish trapped in a confined space, making success virtually guaranteed. The origins of this expression are rooted in the literal sense of the phrase— shooting fish in a barrel is indeed quite effortless. Its earliest recorded use in writing can be traced back to the 19th century, often associated with humorous anecdotes or hyperbolic descriptions. Over time, the idiom has expanded beyond its literal context to depict any situation that presents minimal challenge due to the overwhelming advantage or simplicity involved. Today, we use it both playfully and pragmatically to highlight tasks that require little effort, often eliciting a knowing smile from those who understand the inherent ease of the task at hand.

402. Make a long story short

The idiom "make a long story short" succinctly conveys the act of summarizing or condensing a lengthy narrative into its essential points, skipping unnecessary details to get to the core of the matter. It's like trimming down a sprawling tale into a concise and impactful version. While its precise origins are unclear, this phrase has been in use since at least the 16th century, reflecting the human inclination to simplify stories for efficiency. Over time, its meaning has remained consistent, evolving to accommodate our fast-paced communication styles. Today, we use this expression to swiftly transition from a detailed explanation to a brief conclusion, emphasizing brevity and ensuring our audience grasps the main idea without getting lost in the intricacies of a protracted narrative. It's a linguistic shortcut that keeps conversations engaging and to the point.

403. Off the beaten path

The idiom "off the beaten path" paints a picturesque scene of venturing away from the commonly traveled route, exploring uncharted territory or unconventional experiences. It's like straying from the well-trodden trail to discover hidden gems or unique adventures. Its origins are metaphorical, drawing parallels to the literal practice of choosing lesser-known trails while hiking. Though pinpointing its first use in writing is challenging, the idiom gained prominence in the 20th century, signifying a departure from the ordinary. Over time, its meaning has extended beyond physical journeys to encompass any situation where one seeks novel or unconventional avenues, often driven by a desire for authenticity or discovery. Today, we use this phrase to suggest embracing the unfamiliar, celebrating the spirit of adventure and the thrill of encountering the unexpected. It's an invitation to step beyond the routine and embrace the allure of the unknown.

404. One man's trash is another man's treasure

The idiom "one man's trash is another man's treasure" refers to the concept that what might be deemed worthless by one person could hold immense value for another. It's like highlighting the subjectivity of worth and the diverse ways in which individuals perceive and appreciate items or experiences. Its origins trace back to the 17th century, when John Ray penned "One man's meat is another man's poison," which inspired the modern adaptation. Over time, the idiom's scope has broadened beyond material possessions to symbolize the uniqueness of individual preferences and perspectives. Today, we use this expression to celebrate diversity, encourage open-mindedness, and remind us that there's beauty and value in the unexpected or overlooked. It's an acknowledgment of the varied ways we assign meaning to the world around us, fostering a sense of appreciation for differing viewpoints.

Bonus!

1144 Random Facts

Thanks for supporting me and purchasing this book! I'd like to send you some freebies. They include:

- The digital version of *500 World War I & II Facts*

- The digital version of *101 Idioms and Phrases*

- The audiobook for my best seller

Scan the **QR** code below, enter your email and I'll send you all the files. Happy reading!

Find more of me on Amazon!

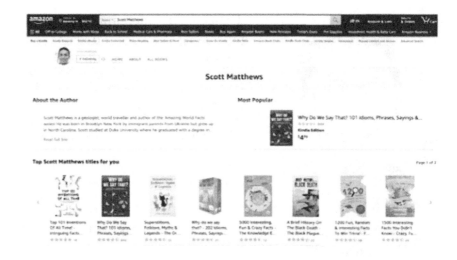

Check out the "Amazing Facts" series and learn more about the world around us!

Made in the USA
Coppell, TX
20 December 2023

26676066R00262